Identity and Belonging: The African Others in South Africa

Authors
Vivian Ojong
Stephen Basure

Langaa Research & Publishing CIG
Mankon, Bamenda

Publisher:
Langaa RPCIG
Langaa Research & Publishing Common Initiative Group
P.O. Box 902 Mankon
Bamenda
North West Region
Cameroon
Langaagrp@gmail.com
www.langaa-rpcig.net

Distributed in and outside N. America by African Books Collective
orders@africanbookscollective.com
www.africanbookscollective.com

ISBN-10: 9956-553-09-3
ISBN-13: 978-9956-553-09-9

Ojong, Vivian

Professor Vivian Ojong is a Full Professor in the Discipline of Anthropology, at the College of Humanities University of KwaZulu-Natal (UKZN), Durban, South Africa. She is currently the Dean and Head of the School of Social Science and the Interim Dean of Research for the College of Humanities at the University of KwaZulu-Natal, Durban. Professor Ojong's research areas are identity politics, migration and internationalization, globalization and diaspora studies, gender, feminism, research methodology and methods, entrepreneurship as well as culture and religion. She has successfully completed the supervision of 17 Doctoral (Ph.D.) and a number of Masters Students, mentored 7 Postdoctoral Fellows, and published 54 research articles as journal articles, two edited books, and book chapters. Professor Ojong has examined a number of Masters and Ph.D. theses from various Universities including the University of Fort Hare and the University of Nelson Mandela Metropolitan University, University of Cape Town, University of Free State, Walter Sisulu University. She is a reviewer for many high-impact factor journals and Guest Editor of some Special Issues. Professor Ojong is a National Research Foundation (NRF), South Africa rated social scientist since 2018.

Basure, Stephen

Dr Stephen Basure is a holder of a PHD in Anthropology from the University of Pretoria. He is a Postdoctoral Research Fellow at the University of KwaZulu-Natal where he has undertaken research since 2022. He has been in the academic field for the past 13 years and has taught several modules and research supervision at both undergraduate and postgraduate levels. His research interests lie in mobility, marginality, and contemporary forms of inclusion, and exclusion. He has undertaken research and published several works on migration, forced displacement as well as marginality and post migration experiences of communities. Currently, he is working on research on issues of migration and citizenship in South Africa.

DHA	Department of Home Affairs
DZP	Documentation Zimbabwean Project
LSP	Lesotho Special Permit
SADC	Southern African Development Community
ZEP	Zimbabwe Exemption Permit

Table of Contents

Acknowledgements

This book is a product of collaborative efforts of various individuals who shared their ideas, resources, motivation, encouragement, and cooperation to make the project successful. We are hugely indebted to everyone who has made this project a success. We would like to appreciate the migrants who agreed to be part of the book. Conversations of identity and belonging stir personal reflections and leads to questioning of some uncomfortable truths about migrant lives. We are grateful to the African migrants who have allowed us to peep into their lives and to document their day-to-day experiences of living in foreign spaces. The book has been made possible through their openness in sharing what it means to be an African foreigner in South Africa. We also appreciate the great work done by the reviewers who took their time to go through the manuscript and provided insightful guidance on the articulation of ideas.

Reflections on our personal experiences in both the academic journeys and living in South Africa, and the desire to continuously reconceptualise and rethink issues of identity and belonging in the context of migration has been part of our conversations. These desires have given birth to this book as we continuously find ways to make sense of the dynamics of migration in South Africa. In Sub Saharan Africa, South Africa remains a major migrant destination, resulting in the continuous growth of communities of African migrants in the country. This has created interesting dynamics on both the level of policy making and academic theorising on the migration frameworks.

We therefore combine a historical policy analysis approach and ethnographic fieldwork to provide perspectives of the identity and belonging of African others in South Africa. This enabled us to have an appreciation of the changing trends of migration discourses in post-apartheid South Africa. Through interrogating the citizenship of African others, we discuss how issues of identity and belonging shape the ways in which foreign African migrants integrate into South African society. Academic works on migration have noted the processes of policymaking, control and conflicts characterising migration discourses, and we hope our book contributes further to the capturing of migrant experiences and sentiments about being the African other as well as to theorising migration in South Africa.

Vivian Ojong
Dean and Head of School of Social Sciences

Stephen Basure
Postdoctoral Fellow in the School of Social Sciences
University of KwaZulu-Natal
South Africa

Chapter 1

Citizenship and Belonging in South Africa

Introduction

Migration trends are growing across Africa and the world. As drivers of migration continue to be characteristic of different spaces and influencing people to be on the move, the dynamics of migration continue to assume different facets. This book delves into the subject of citizenship and belonging. As the world continues along a trajectory of circulation of migrants, the twin questions of citizenship and belonging are indispensable to the contemporary discussions of migration. How people settle and integrate within societies across the world has been a topical issue evoking fears of both migrants and their hosts. These fears range from claims of insecurity, cultural and moral erosion, competition over economic resources and livelihoods as well as a general fear of an unprecedented immigrant influx in host communities. This creates a climate that shapes issues of citizenship and belonging. The legal and policy frameworks relating to migration have underlying tones that reflect the vision and fears of most host societies. They spell out the unwritten perceptions regarding the migration process. There are several questions that are raised in the minds of both migrants and hosts. For the hosts, the questions relate to the degree of openness and the limits of their accommodation of migrants, whereas for the migrants, the degree of permanence or whether to be on the move again becomes their greatest question. It shapes their investment commitment and ultimately feelings of belonging. The situation produces a quagmire.

The uncertainties characteristic of the migration process and the regulation of migration present dilemmas and a terrain that is difficult to navigate both theoretically and practically. In a way it produces a quagmire and epistemological nightmare. Several aspects influence the shape of this quagmire. For the migrant, it stems from the complex drivers of the migration process. Mostly foreign African migrants have settled in contemporary South Africa due to the country being the best migration destination in the region in terms of opportunities and avenues for earning livelihoods. On the other hand, there are complex home forces that drive the migrants out and force them to find locations that promise the best options for them (Crush, Williams and Peberdy, 2005). However, the migrants encounter a myriad of challenges, including cumbersome entry requirements and delayed decision makings on their applications. On finally getting into South Africa, they have to deal with the everyday realities of living in a foreign country. We therefore endeavour to document the melting pot of migrants' experiences and how they shape their experience of belonging. Migration scholars have also attempted to theorise and conceptualize the nature and character of the migration discourse in South Africa (Posel 2004, Landau 2011, Makina and Mudungwe, 2023). The crosscutting analyses have sought to proffer ways of seeing migration from different angles and perhaps be able to offer sound epistemological responses to the phenomenon. This book adds to the analysis of citizenship and belonging in contemporary South Africa. The contemporary struggles over citizenship focusing specifically on migrant African foreigners in South Africa are examined.

Migration in Context

Migration in Southern Africa, as elsewhere in the world, has been an integral feature of societies. Due to regional economic inequalities and different favourable conditions, South Africa has emerged to be the most favoured destination for the bulk of African migrants in contemporary times. There is a widely held notion that South Africa has the richest economy hence most Africans continue to seek good fortunes and perhaps establish permanent residence in the country (Rugunanan and Xulu-Gama, 2022; Ojong and Sithole, 2007; Ojong, 2005). Since the colonial era Migration patterns have been unstable in Southern Africa, with migrants travelling mostly to find employment in the mining, agricultural and construction sectors in most of the region (Crush and Peberdy, 2005). The fall of colonisation and apartheid has also shifted the dynamics of migration. Coupled with postcolonial governance dynamics and political turmoil, as well as economic troubles and poverty, South Africa has been the dominant destination for most migrants (Batisai, 2022). The continued migrant inflows into South Africa continue to raise questions of citizenship, inclusiveness, and otherness. Whilst this is not a new question, the book creates a new opportunity to incorporate fresh perspectives and a new lens through which to understand current belonging questions in South Africa. Most scholars have focused on the driving factors shaping migration, community integration and adaptation of migrants into the South African nation, and policy frameworks, xenophobia, Afrophobia as responses to the 'migrant problem' (Misago and Landau, 2023; Rugunanan and Xulu-Gama, 2022; Mhandu, Ojong and Muzvidziwa, 2018). However, this book offers ethnographic perspectives of self-definition and perceptions of belonging of foreign African migrants in South Africa. On the theoretical level, the attempt is to show how the organisation and distribution of resources continue to be a central feature structuring migrant patterns, and the responses to it. It is a running thread informing both official and local responses to migration. Official responses are seen through the changing frameworks of policies and legislation aimed at controlling migration patterns whilst the local responses may be understood through the everyday interaction of African migrants and the communities they live in.

Understanding citizenship and belonging

Perhaps the departing point of endeavours to understand migration is to put the concepts of citizenship and belonging into context. The idea of political citizenship deals mostly with the relationship between the individual and the state. It identifies the formal statutes and regulations that govern this relationship. Belonging deals with the qualitative issues of emotions and feelings relating to the link with a community and society. These two concepts are important as they influence the migration process, and they provide insights into the discourse on migration. An examination of the concept of citizenship presents complex dynamics in relation to its nature, origins, and character. Although the simplistic political conceptions of citizenship appear to drive major understandings of the concept, scholars have noted varying conceptions and parameters of understanding citizenship. Wegner (2014) notes varying forms of citizenship including but not limited to national citizenship, economic citizenship and social citizenship. These derivatives threaten the unitary parochial perceptions of citizenship which has been conceptualised as a status, an identity, and an idea (Wegner, 2014; Heater, 2006). It assumes different usages making it a fluid concept that needs to be stabilised by contextual reference to specific aspects such as discussions of belonging. However, in this book two complexities are addressed These are the problems of legality encased in the concept of national citizenship and the social citizenship characterised by the internal interactive dynamics of migrants and hosts.

Contemporary manifestations of citizenship are influenced by different situations. There are conditions that trigger discussions of citizenship. These include moments of crisis, issues of migration and immigration, as well as the resultant migrant host interactions (Wegner, 2014). As contemporary issues of migration continue to influence discussions of citizenship, the twin issues of globalism and decoloniality shape citizenship discourses in Africa. The scholarly discourse is punctuated by arguments that try to understand citizenship in the different situations mentioned above. The issues of context continue to change with every epoch being marked by specific configurations of citizenship. However, Lonsdale's condensation of the central ideas of citizenship reduces the phenomenon to three basic issues (Lonsdale, 2016). These include eligibility, costs, and the benefits of citizenship. Eligibility relates to answering the question of who qualifies to be a citizen whilst on the other hand the issue of cost relates to what one must give to gain citizenship. It describes the obligations of the citizen and the duties of loyalty to the state. The last aspect of benefits looks at the kinds of benefits that flow to the citizen in terms of the freedoms and services that the state can provide. As noted by Lonsdale (2016), the conditions for the satisfaction of these issues of citizenship are always changing in terms of both who can become the citizen and the mutual benefits that flow between the state and the individual. There is a continued narrowing of the categories of eligibility and defining who the stranger is. An historical approach to the concept of citizenship is explored in the following section which seeks to align understandings of citizenship in the African context.

Historical perspectives on citizenship

The idea of citizenship has been around since ancient civilizations and the evolution of the ideas of states and nationhood. It came as a concept regulating obligations, expectations, and rights of individuals in relation to space and authority (Haklay et al., 2021; Kochenov, 2019). Hence different regimes of authority had a bearing on the nature and character of citizenship. Without resorting to a historical rewriting of the historical evolution of citizenship, this section seeks to specifically weave an African perspective on citizenship and how it influences contemporary configurations of the relationship between the state and the individual. This is crucial in charting a niche on the rights and experiences of African migrants as they seek to access rights in foreign spaces. In African states, citizenship should be understood within three historical epochs i.e., the precolonial, colonial, and postcolonial periods. Apart from this periodisation, the idea and phenomenon of globalisation should also be understood to see its implications on the configurations of citizenship in contemporary African states. In all the stages of societal evolution, the important aspect is understanding the ways in which changing contexts configure issues of citizenship and belonging. Contexts determine and influence the emergence of criteria for selecting who can be citizen and the characteristics of the relationship between the individual and authority. Moreover, the insider/outsider dichotomy is constantly undergoing changes to mirror the prevailing societal forces. The ways in which these conditions continue to play out in contemporary South Africa are explored.

During the precolonial era, the issue of belonging can be understood by utilising the concepts of ethnicity and belonging, and later the aspects of political structures characterising traditional states (Kornegay, 2006). Ethnicity could be seen to be a major organising principle, with people being accepted based on their descent (Hunter, 2016). The modern conception of citizenship was non-existent as rights and obligations were negotiated within different political formations, and configurations of belonging were mediated through ethnicity and other dynamics. Although issues of discrimination were rare, dominant groups often engaged in the creation of classes where people outside their ethnic identity could become subjects, whose presence was tied to their willingness to recognise authority, and mostly pay tribute to the authority of the dominant groups. Hunter (2016) notes that precolonial African societies were always on the move, something which is seen as being reconfigured with the coming in of the nation-state during the colonial era. In adopting a loose definition of citizenship during the precolonial era, Hunter (2016) notes that struggles for citizenship were struggles for incorporation. Notwithstanding the power differentials, the ruler and the subjects were locked in a mutual relationship of exchange where the subjects wanted the benefits of incorporation whereas the ruler required subjects over which to exercise power. People could simply leave political systems that no longer served their interests (Lonsdale, 2016).

Colonialism should be seen as the major determinant of current configurations of citizenship due to its creation of modern day African national boundary systems (Dorman, Hammett and Nugent, 2007; Nyamnjoh, 2008). These boundaries still determine the national dynamics in all African states and establish definite areas of jurisdiction. Colonial political systems did not accept the citizenship of Africans, rather relegating them to subjects who had to accept the laws set by the minority colonising regimes. Africans did not possess any significant rights, and were often regarded as property that could be used to sustain the colonial economies. Issues of forced labour, extortionate taxation, and dispossessions of space for Africans were the hallmarks of colonial governance (Kornegay, 2006; Nyamnjoh 2008). Perhaps colonialism can be credited for creating the dual systems of citizenship and subjectification where African communities were mostly treated as colonial subjects who were devoid of any rights. The white minority enjoyed citizenship rights, whilst the Africans were treated as sub humans who could not afford to have rights. In the South African case, it is notable that the apartheid regime was not open to the idea of African citizenship, hence the design of constitutional provisions that were silent on the position of African citizenship (Manby, 2009). Most Africans had to engage in violent struggles to gain both recognition as citizens as well as access to power. However, the postcolonial state has faced insurmountable challenges in conquering the ghost of the colonial nation-state. Despite wide ranging attempts at creating the African citizen, the concept of nationalism has emerged to be stronger and a ready tool for politicians who tend to benefit from the anti-African unity message (Hunter, 2016). Although Kornegay (2006) notes the solidarity of African regional bodies, their success in rethinking the nationalistic conception of citizenship remains problematic. Post coloniality and decoloniality are ongoing ideological standpoints that influence contemporary arguments on citizenship. The calls for an African citizen reflect a desire to transcend colonial configurations of citizenship by appealing to the African identity.

Legislating citizenship

The idea of legislating citizenship involves the process by which a country creates legal and policy frameworks governing who is considered to be a citizen and what rights and responsibilities they have within that nation (Sadiq, 2008). This typically involves enacting citizenship laws, immigration laws and naturalisation processes. In the context of South Africa, legislation related to citizenship is primarily governed by the South African Citizenship Act of 1995. This Act outlines the conditions under which individuals can acquire and renounce South African citizenship. The acquisition of citizenship in South Africa is through birth, descent, and naturalisation. The South African state pursues a strict regime of defining and recognising the citizenship in relation to perceived others. Outside the parameters of birth and descent, the naturalisation requirements of perceived outsiders are complex and ever-changing. Since the fall of apartheid, South Africa has gone through several regimes of citizenship acquisition regulations which streamline and tighten the ability of foreign African migrants to acquire citizenship (Klaaren, 2008; Muzondidya, 2010). The space for outsiders to acquire citizenship is closing as the state pursues an inward-looking law and policymaking framework (Moyo and Zanker, 2020). Chapter three of the book attempts to provide a wide-ranging discussion on the legal frameworks governing citizenship in South Africa. various dynamics have emerged that structure the ways in which citizenship is acquired in contemporary South Africa. As discussed by Moyo and Zanker (2020), there is an increased securitisation of migration, noted through increased legislation and the policing of migration processes. The launch of the Border Management Authority cements this perspective of securitisation, whereas the Gauteng province has seen the increased surveillance of migrants by police. Legislation has been noted to build a wall around citizenship, by creating a thick barrier between insiders and outsiders (Sadiq, 2008).

Anthropological discourses on belonging

Schama (1995), defines belonging as a sense of experience, a phenomenology of locality which serves to create, mould, and reflect perceived ideals around the place. Connerton, (1989) noted the empirical context and origins of belonging as intrinsically linked to how loyalties are created, perpetuated, and modified. This relationship in turn informs an understanding of belonging not only in the sense of locality but also of individual relationships. The idea of belonging has undergone several conceptualisations in Anthropology. It is a multifaceted concept that incorporates social, cultural, personal, and other factors in the relationships of individuals to space. Some of the key features of belonging include cultural identity, social integration rituals and symbols, and inclusion and exclusion. Belonging determines who can have access to what types of resources in society. It informs distinctions between cultural groups and may influence a propagation of conflict where multiple claims of belonging are made. In the context of migration, the idea of belonging gives rise to questions of place and space (Muzondidya, 2010; Abu El-Haj, 2019). Migrants in the diaspora have to deal with balancing their need to be tied to new spaces as well as their connection to their roots. Migration brings new contexts of practice in relation to belonging. Most Anthropologists have also conceptualised belonging within the context of identity. The issues of identity and belonging are discussed in the next section. As noted by Landau and Blakewell (2018), Africa is characterised by the movement of people within the continent. The varied ethnic and linguistic differences should be seen as conditions that stimulate an emergence of people out of place. Hence this book attempts to move beyond the traditional factors motivating migration cycles through concentrating on the dynamics of settlement and belonging of foreign African migrants in South Africa. Discourses of diversity attempt to welcome differences and celebrate them, whilst contemporary parochial standpoints advocate assimilation, sameness, and blending in by requiring migrant integration into host communities.

The concept of 'home' has been used as an analytical tool in Anthropological discourses of migration and belonging. It helps in capturing individual connections to space by examining their construction of space and attachment. It brings out the qualitative aspects of emotional connections, a sense of security and comfort. It evokes the idea of being settled and a space where one feels at home. In the concept of home, ideas of belonging are captured. For Ojong (2012), home is the place where an individual feels emotionally fulfilled and physically secure on a symbolic level. This characterisation of home speaks succinctly to the issue of belonging and enlightens on how belonging is symbolically and emotionally created. A migrant may inhabit a foreign space for a considerable time but still live in a transient mode without feeling attached to the migration space. Research on migration has explored the concepts of transnationalism and the linkages between migrants and their places of origin. These dynamics enable an understanding of the construction of belonging amongst migrants. Whereas some migrants integrate and accept the changing conditions of their living, other migrants engage in the politics of waiting, looking at their situations as temporary whilst they wait for the conditions in their home country to improve. The politics of waiting is characterised by the hope of a return, with migrants foreseeing a future return, either upon accumulating wealth, retirement, or socioeconomic change (Stasik, Hänsch, and Mains, 2020; Candiz and Belanger, 2019). Elements of investments in their countries of origin display a deeper connection with home whilst the migrant location is viewed as a stepping stone to the achievement of a desired socioeconomic improvement. The book deals with constructions of home in Chapter 5 as it explores migrant interactions with space and community in South Africa.

Identity and belonging

Identity and belonging are important aspects of the process of migration. Migration brings people from different localities into contact by engendering diversity. This can result in various conflicts along identity lines. Africa is characterised by multiculturalism that is a direct outcome of the colonial process that influenced the drawing of national boundaries which grouped together individuals belonging to different ethnic groups thereby fostering a multi-ethnic society. These multi-ethnic societies have often been characterised by ethnic differences and conflicts. The migration of foreign African migrants becomes an important aspect that adds to already existing ethnic dimensions (Landau and Bakewell, 2018). It contributes to the melting pot of identities. These identities are crucial in determining the access to resources. identity is tied to a complex web of societal markers that constitute part and parcel of how politics of being are internally and externally resolved. Debates on identity and belonging have often toyed with the idea that societies are born out of national cultural homogeneity, a phenomenon that influenced perceptions that migrants must assimilate or blend in with the receiving communities (O'Reilly, 2022). However, the internal differences within receiving communities present interesting dimensions of identities in the context of migration. To better understand the dynamics, the following is an excerpt from the story of one African migrant in Durban. Paul has been in Durban since 2008 and has been employed at different companies. However, for the past three years he has been employed in an international organisation based in Durban and their work involves travelling and interacting with communities. Paul notes that the climate at the organisation is complex due to the multiplicity of identities among the workers. His team is composed of white expatriates, a Venda speaker from the Limpopo Province, a Sepedi speaker from Gauteng as well as two local isiZulu speakers. This context of differences exposes the internal inconsistencies of identity. The people speaking IsiZulu, Venda and Sepedi are all identified as indigenous South Africans, but Paul notes that they cannot converse with each other in local languages due to their differences. Hence they have all resorted to the English language as a standard communication tool. For Paul as a foreign African migrant, this situation is advantageous since he does not have to struggle fitting in as there has been a standardisation of communication to deal with the problems of internal cultural differences. From this conversation, issues of identity are seen to be tied to contexts and place. Those who might have the 'legitimate' claim to belonging are characterised by difference which makes their identities become based on differences and multiple reference points. Identity and belonging hence become negotiated factors, where insiderness and outsiderness are continuously subject to negotiation (Lemanski, 2020). Paul's outsiderness is less pronounced due to the multi-ethnic environment at his workplace.

Paul's situation also raises fundamental questions about belonging. The usage of identity as a marker of belonging is complex. There are multiple factors that affect how identity is constructed and how that culminates in regimes of connections with space. Using physical features and names may not be simple tools to distinguish foreign African migrants from locals. The question of who the South African citizen is becomes problematic as multiple factors have to be considered when it comes to the formulation of the South African identity (Ramphele, 2001; Mosselson, 2010; Muzondidya, 2010). The insider/outsider debate is also more about personal formulations of identity and self-definition. The migration process implies population movement, uprooting individuals from their reference points of identity. Place, culture, community, language and other aspects of identities are redefined in foreign spaces. Migrants have to negotiate new reference points, hence the imperative of examining how they experience belonging in the areas to which they migrate. Belonging stems from the experiential dynamics of attachment to place and these are also negotiated by the internal factors of the individual as well as the outside climate of local attitudes towards the migrant.

Bridging the Divide: Dealing with Difference

Emerging scholarship has dwelt more on ways of adapting and settling in among migrants in South Africa. Chekero and Morreira (2020) discuss the functionality of convivial relations that exploit the concept of friendship to mediate migrants access to resources and livelihoods in South Africa. Writing about Zimbabwean migrants, Chekero and Morreira (2020), note the importance of trans ethnic and transnational friendship in enabling migrant access to South African communities, even in the context of broader national anti-immigrant sentiments and attitudes. It is the day-to-day interactions and relationships that structure the belonging of migrants. By appealing to individual personal relationships, migrants are able to negotiate the difficulties that are imposed by anti-immigrant sentiments. However, although convivial relationships enable getting by, they do not explore the deeper levels of belonging. The perceptions of temporariness may fuel certain attitudes where migrants establish relationships for the purpose of getting by without investing into the permanence of settlement. The perceptions and feelings of belonging for migrants should be understood in the broader context of how they interpret their presence, their relationship with their roots and their outlook reflected in their visions, aspirations, and future plans. Daily experiences and encounters with various contexts of the community contribute to their experience of foreignness whilst individual networks and relationships may enable negotiations that allow getting by and surviving in foreign spaces. Belonging often results in feelings of permanence and settling, and an outlook that confirms feeling more attached to certain spaces (Ojong, 2012).

Discussions of conviviality also reflect agentic reactions to the broader structural constraints. Whilst the broader outlook of emigration may be characterised by official stifling of migration, it is the personal and individualistic connections that fuel migration and belonging in constrained spaces. Landau and Bakewell (2018) note the collusion of migrants, hosts, politicians and other actors as redefining contexts of migration and enabling the renegotiation and navigation of migration. Although legality may be a major issue, individuals engage in various behaviours to respond to the situation. From intermarriages, opening businesses and clandestine access to legal documents, individual level interactions enable regimes of migration to survive various structural constraints. Greater migration control only increases the cost of access rather than discouraging the existence of migration. It results in inequalities in relation to their access to social and economic capital that enables them to continue living in migrant spaces.

Methodology

The book is organised around the three broad areas of focus which are discussed in the following sections. Its broad aims are to rekindle thoughts, ideas, and analyses of experiences in citizenship in South Africa. Issues of belonging continue to be central to these questions and the changing economic, political, and social dynamics continue to reshape the terrain of this citizenship. The three broad areas discussed in this book include understanding citizenship, identity and belonging, theorising on citizenship, and experiences of citizenship in South Africa. The book deals with the following questions:

1. What constitutes a citizen in South Africa?
2. What are the experiences of migrant Africans in integrating into South African communities?
3. What are the policy changes in post-apartheid South Africa in relation to citizenship, and how have these shaped discourses on citizenship for African migrants?
4. Is the South African community ready for the citizenship of African migrants?

To answer these questions, the book takes the reader through a journey of understanding of how issues of citizenship and belonging for African migrants are structured. This is done through taking a historical journey that traces issues of citizenship, policy changes and contemporary dynamics of migrant lives in South Africa.

Apart from the historical reviews, the book was based on a multi-sited ethnographic approach to understand the experiences of African migrants in South Africa. Primary data for some of the Chapters was obtained from interviews, conversations and multiple interactions with African migrants based in different localities in South Africa. The study drew from respondents based in multiple selected sites within South Africa. Multi-sited ethnography is a method of collecting data that follows a social problem across different field sites that are geographically and/or socially determined. Much of the twentieth century anthropological thinking identified the field as a single site to which the ethnographer went and from which he/she returned. This constituted a key element in the ethos of anthropological research, which emphasised contextual understanding and relevance towards a particular social phenomenon under investigation. Towards the end of the twentieth century, some scholars began arguing for multi-stranded approaches in studying and interpreting various social phenomena. Multi-sited ethnography was proposed as a research model to collapse the distinction between the local site and the global system (Marcus, 1995). This new development challenges the separation of the 'field site' as the province of the ethnographer from the global systemic realities through which local knowledge should be understood. Purposive sampling was employed to purposefully select relevant respondents in the study. Snowballing sampling will also be used to complement the selection of the respondents. This is mostly because migrants often create specific communities with other migrants, and being introduced to these communities requires referral and trust. Unstructured interviews analysis was the major tool for data collection.

Structure of the Book

The book consists of six Chapters that address the interrelated concepts of citizenship and belonging. The first chapter contextualizes citizenship and belonging in South Africa: This chapter gives an introductory overview and definitional issues on citizenship and belonging in the African context. It also sets out the outline of the book and prepares the reader to get a grasp and direction on issues of belonging and identity. The Chapter also sets out the tones and the major arguments of the book. Methodological issues are also explained in this Chapter. In chapter 2 a theoretical grounding of the belonging of the African others is presented. The Chapter deals with theoretical arguments surrounding belonging and citizenship. It explores how this theorisation can help to understand the context of belonging in South Africa. It looks at anthropological aspect of ordering and its focus on otherness to show how this has shaped the creation of perceptions towards citizenship and belonging. The Chapter also examines the sociological aspect of ordering societies and how this underlies approaches towards citizenship and belonging. The theoretical arguments explored are structured around three themes i.e., control, positioning and resources. These shape the view of migration dynamics in South Africa. The identified standpoints allow a better comprehension of how the discourses of belonging in South Africa have been structured currently and historically.

In chapter 3 a review of immigration policies in South Africa is provided. This Chapter focuses on an evolutionary/historical approach to the question of belonging and citizenship of African migrants. It proceeds from a thorough documentation of migration trends and perceptions towards African minds in South African policy and practice. The Chapter attempts to take stock of the conditions which have structured migration to South Africa by Africans and understand how policy changes informed the construction of perceptions towards African migrants. The Chapter also focuses on the changing conceptions of belonging in policy and in practice. It investigates the issue of citizenship and attempts to answer the question of who can become an African citizen. It explores the different forms that structure access to South African citizenship by African migrants, through focusing on policy and legal requirements underlying citizenship acquisition in different historical epochs. The legal dynamics of citizenship acquisition are analysed. Chapter 4 presents the experiences of African others with legal frameworks of accessing citizenship in South Africa. The chapter examines the changing nature of citizenship in South Africa and examines contemporary struggles over citizenship by African migrants in post-apartheid South Africa. Differential treatment of African migrants is explored (Zimbabwe Special Permit, Lesotho Pass). The Chapter also explores continuity and change in the legality of African migrants. It provides narratives and everyday struggles of foreign African migrants as they negotiate access to citizenship in South Africa.

In Chapter 5 community experiences of the belonging of foreign African migrants is explored. This Chapter explores belonging by looking into the everyday interactions of migrants and their host communities. The daily practices and how they shape the landscape for the propagation of feelings of belonging for foreign African migrants are explored. Several aspects including the public sphere, living dynamics and work and financial dynamics are analysed to bring out how they are integral in the formation of feelings of belonging among migrants in South Africa.

Chapter 6 concludes by revisiting the important question of the citizenship and belonging of African others in South Africa. The focus of this chapter is exploring the question, can a migrant African be a South African citizen? It is a reflection on the contemporary and historical discourses of citizenship and belonging in South Africa and attempts to put struggles over belonging into perspective. The Chapter gives concluding remarks through revisiting the questions of belonging, using and basing the arguments on a combination of the historical, theoretical, and experiential dynamics of foreign African migrants in South Africa

Conclusion

This chapter examined and conceptualised the aspects of citizenship and belonging. It sets out the key arguments in perspective through providing a conceptual basis of understanding citizenship and belonging. Citizenship relates to formalities of the relations between the individual and the state. It is tied to legalities and aspects of mutual obligations between the two parties. The phenomenon of migration sets the stage for acceptance that is negotiated in the concept of belonging. The Chapter notes that the idea of belonging for the migrant transcends the issues of legality and become more pronounced in the negotiation and renegotiation of identity in the public sphere. However, conceptions of legality are important in shaping the mood of where the foreign African migrants have to negotiate belonging. The Chapter has raised important questions about migration, citizenship and belonging. The question of how citizenship is constructed is important in the understanding of contemporary struggles for legality among migrants in South Africa. It explains the various issues of the formal regulation of migration and how this structures the climate for negotiating belonging. The chapters in the book present a broadened understanding of citizenship built upon an appreciation of state migrant relations and migrant community interactions. Discourses of legality, rights and experiences ultimately shape the interpretation and understanding of the concepts of citizenship and belonging. In the next chapter, we explore the theoretical aspects of understanding the identity and belonging of African others in South Africa. Identity and belonging are issues that are shaped by multiple issues, hence the need for a theoretical focus that enables an appreciation of the ways in which identity and belonging discourses are shaped by multiple factors in South Africa.

Chapter 2

Theorising Belonging

Introduction

This Chapter deals with theoretical arguments surrounding belonging and citizenship. It explores how this theorisation can help in understanding the context of belonging in South Africa. It looks at the anthropological aspect of ordering and its focus on otherness to show how this has shaped the creation of perceptions towards citizenship and belonging. The Chapter also examines the sociological aspect of ordering societies and how this underlies approaches towards citizenship and belonging. The theoretical arguments explored will also include strategic essentialism, instrumentalism, functionalism, and the frustration aggression theory. These will be examined to help understand how they shape the understanding of discourses of belonging in South Africa. The theoretical standpoints presented in this section must be understood in relation to their role in the analysis of different aspects of the migration experience. The first aspect relates to the issue of managing the migration flow. The answer to the question of who gets accepted is crucial in the management of migration. Moreover, it addresses the rights and obligations of the migrants as they settle in South Africa. Several theorisations have emerged in relation to the process of how migrants are accepted into South Africa, and the motivations behind the patterns of migration flow. Managing migration also points to the feelings of authority and abilities of management on the part of the state and its agencies. The state as the sovereign authority creates mechanisms of governance that reflect its abilities to handle the migration problems. Policies reflect the various beliefs of authorities in relation to how they perceive to be in control of the situation.

The second issue that the theoretical arguments outlined here is the dynamics of migrant interactions as they settle in the host communities. Relations between hosts and migrants are structured by various elements. There is conflict, competition, and cooperation.

These multiple viewpoints require theorisation to explain the behaviours of different parties related to the migration processes. Certain ways of behavioural patterns which emerge out of the migration experience are addressed. These reflect the attitudes of the different stakeholders locked together by the migration process. Units of analysis that basically cover three dimensions of the migration experiences are presented. First are at the dynamics of power and control and how they play out in different political dispensations. By adopting the concept of the cultures of ordering, how migration management creates the desire for the state to exert control over the migration process is explored. There are various avenues for the experience of state power in the migration process. This includes an analysis of laws and policies, and the implementation of legal statutes regulation on the lives of the migrants. Secondly, how migrant host competition is framed in the context of access is looked at. Access is an important concept that structures struggles for transformation and change in society. Within those struggles, individuals and groups strategically position themselves to succeed and get the best out of the situation. By borrowing the concept of strategic essentialism, how essentialising victimhood is part of the game of negotiating access between the migrants and their hosts was analysed. Identities are essentialised to become capital that is influential in determining access.

Lastly, conflicts in the migration process in terms of the struggles over resources are categorised. The psychological conceptualisations of frustration and aggression are used to situate struggles between various parties to the migration experience. Inclusion, exclusion and even violence should be examined mostly in terms of how they are shaped by perceptions towards resource distribution and the barriers for individuals and groups to access those resources. Often scholars have engaged in discussions and theorising on xenophobia and Afrophobia, pointing to the presence of the irrational fears of migrants (Masenya, 2017; Tarisayi and Manik, 2020; Sibanda, 2022). However, there is a rationality to this irrationality. The fears of migrants are borne out of perceptions of scarcity and access and how different groups affect each other's claim to resources. Although these may seem to be aspects unrelated to citizenship, citizenship and belonging occur within specific frameworks that shape the experiences of individuals and groups. Perceptions and attitudes on the migration experience are shaped at the points of interaction. In the following sections, the various theoretical standpoints that allow an understanding of the migration process are discussed.

Ordering Society: the quest for managing migration

Migrant management is born out of the desire to create and establish ordered societies. While it has been noted that human mobility is as old as humanity itself, contemporary discourses focus mainly on the containment of individuals. Ideas of identity space, and belonging are part and parcel of an elaborate attempt at ordering societies today. Creation of borders, visa regimes and documentation are all attempts to ensure full control and understanding of who is where and accounting for individuals. Looking at the South African migration context, there is evidence of attempts to ensure that officials are aware of who the migrants are and where they are in order to establish regimes of control over them. This has always created a difficult and costly situation due to the difficulties in creating clear avenues for migrant accountability. Home Affairs minister Aaron Motsoaledi noted in one of his interviews, "how can you document someone when they don't want to be documented" (SABC News Interview). This reflects complexities surrounding the processes and attempts to tame the migrant flows. Order and a sense of control, although desirable, are difficult to put in place in the field of managing populations.

The concept of citizenship should also be seen in the context of the strategies of trying to confine and define people in relation to spaces they occupy (Sadiq, 2008). It also follows a false notion that individuals must earn their citizenship due to the perceived benefits that they offer to the society where they want to settle. Whereas some countries dangle citizenship as rewards and trinkets to award to people with specific qualities, it is argued that citizenship has been used as a tool to control access to space by foreign migrants and to reward those who seem to positively contribute to the host communities. Citizenship discourses in South Africa can be seen to be tied to territory, and hence primarily subject to enforcement of a legal order based on South African territorial rights. The universal discourse of belonging where individuals are expected to have inalienable human rights is replaced by a sovereignty discourse, where citizenship is closely tied to territorial state legislation. Managing migration in South Africa is based upon an elaborate system of inclusion and exclusion. Rights are strictly limited to those who are not regarded as regular migrants. Their experiences are characterised by systematic systems of exclusion from the formal system, as evidenced by strict border entry requirements, sporadic checks on suspected irregular migrants, communication, and financial participation restrictions as well as exclusion from the formal labour market through restrictive measures on the employment of foreigners (Gordon, 2022; Nyamwanza and Dzingirai, 2020). Writing on post-national citizenship in Europe, Kinvall and Nesbitt-Larking (2013) note an increased securitisation of citizenship as well as parallel strategies at de-securitization as migrants engage in various strategies to evade the systematic control. Whilst citizenship across the world is becoming increasingly difficult due to the imposition of several mechanisms which ensure that migrants are in line with national ideals and positively complement the needs of the host communities, there is a pursuit of ordering societies through attempting to govern the migrant qualities and characteristics. Citizenship requirements are bent on ensuring uniformity, regulating behaviour and at least predicting that the immigrant is a good citizen. Migrant profiling starts at points of entry, with contemporary electronic databases of incoming migrants, creating a tool that can be used to enforce a surveillance on the life of the migrant. Hence it should be noted that citizenship restrictions are meant to select and create a perfect candidate for cooption into the host society. This then gives the impression that issues of belonging become easier as individuals with specific qualities and who provide a good fit into the host society are given the privilege of full citizen rights.

Several scholars have explored the issue of order. Order is seen through strategies of organising and regulating society. In terms of migration, the major outcome of the ordering process has been the criminalisation of immigration. Most states have stricter rules governing group membership and discouraging the influx of migrants who are viewed with increasing suspicion and disdain (Barker, 2012; Bourbeau, 2011). Barker (2012) discusses the processes of penalisation and criminalisation of migrants and juxtaposes it with the reassertion of state sovereignty, especially in the face of globalisation. The criminalisation and penalisation of the otherised immigrant often has a bearing on the overall national mood towards migrants. Issues of belonging will have to be negotiated in the context of a mainstreamed discourse of otherising migrants. Legal avenues of citizenship and legality for migrants are tightened, resulting in difficulties with gaining acceptance. Moreover, criminalising migration is a powerful populist strategy which gives the state the ability to label the migrant illegal, influencing the need for strategies for control and elimination of the illegal migrant. State budgets on policing migration have been increasing in major migrant destinations, with moves to control migration flows through tightening and discouraging migration being the major policy stances in relation to migration. The issues of exerting control over foreign African migrants in South Africa evokes feelings of the continuing of the discriminatory policies from the apartheid era.

Perhaps Michel Foucault's work stands out for exploring power, order, and control as well as their use in society, and how this is instrumental in understanding migration management and migrant experiences in host countries. Writing on the panopticon, Foucault (2008), explores the creation of systems of power and how they self-reproduce as individuals seek to avoid overstepping the boundaries set by the surveillance state. Migrants engage in several measures to stay within the parameters of behaviours set out to ensure their eligibility to remain in South Africa. The idea of the panopticon is an adaption of Jeremy Bentham's idea of the Panopticon as a source of power which can influence individual behaviours in several ways (Bentham 2020). The description of the Panopticon given by Michel Foucault creates a situation where an individual is isolated from others whilst he is vulnerable to the gaze of the supervisor situated in the tower. This vulnerability of constantly knowing that you are seen without the ability to see, relate or have companionship, creates an effective isolation ideal for the self-regulation of behaviour by an individual. The exercise of power, according to Foucault, should result in a situation where it is influential whether it is there or not. Just like the design of the panopticon, it creates an impression of the ability to always be seen in the mind of the inmate. At the same time, it does not give an opportunity to verify whether the supervisor is actually watching the inmate. Hence, the design of the panopticon is a design of power which enables impressions of always being in place whether in the presence or absence of an enforcer. Foreign African migrants often feel the unseen coercive power of contemporary migrant systems that exert continuous needs for regularizations and ensuring compliance. The periodic visa applications, the occasional reminder of lapsed accommodation lease agreements and the denial of banking services show the ever-present power of migrant monitoring. The rise of the biometric state seen through the usage of biometric systems of control in migration and border control should also be seen as evidence of the growing power of the surveillance state (Breckenridge, 2005). Just like the apartheid *dompas* system created in the apartheid era, types of surveillance and contemporary forms of biometric regulation continue with similar desires to control population movement. They are part and parcel of ordering and control which has permeated migration dynamics.

The physical architecture of the panopticon has also been seen to be instrumental in ensuring that there is no tyranny, or a centre of power since the one to observe could be anyone. Anyone could enter the centre tower and observe the inmates (Foucault, 2023). This knowledge also shaped the individual conduct of the inmate since he/she is never sure of who is in the observatory, or whether there is actually a person observing. Therefore, the design of the panopticon influences the self-regulation of behaviours. Moreover, the panopticon even allows the supervision of the supervisor himself. It is open to scrutiny and accessible to outsiders like members of the public or other higher authorities. This creates an accountability where the supervisor himself can also be judged from the outside. Thus, the panopticon is applauded by Foucault as a perfect representation of power in society. It is a power which operates without the use of force, but which comes from the anxiety of constantly knowing that one is under surveillance. Migrant lives are often structured through a relative anonymity which instils fear into their interactions with hosts. These influence modes of behaviour that are characterised by a specific form of self-control and regulation so that the migrant avoids actions that may jeopardise their formal presence in South Africa. There are specific ways of deportment and practices of ensuring survival through avoiding anything that may present a reasonable excuse for the revocation of the rights to be in the country. Ordering is an important way of understanding migrant behaviour and their interactions with the public sphere in the areas under study.

Ordering and control of migration not only reflects state power and hegemony. It breeds fear and a culture of hostility towards the whole migration process. It does not allow the separation between the good migrant and the bad migrant. Hence there is a blanket approach to perceptions and moods towards migrants and these ultimately shape the spaces for belonging for the migrant. In the worst case situation, there is a process of dehumanising the migrant, where migrant bodies become 'bodies that do not matter', or what Agamben coins 'disposable bodies' (Agamben and Sacer, 1995; Vandervoodt, 2021). These are characterised by a stripping of the legal protections of certain groups in society. Migrants have often been at a crossroads due to the limitation of their rights and complex processes of negotiating legality in foreign spaces. Their lives are characterised by the occasional disruptions and surveillance under the guise of dealing with illegal migrants. They have to be prepared to prove their legality at different times, and this creates patterns of practice that regulate migrant movement, settlement and interaction in the public sphere. In a way, the regulation and policing of migration produces cultures of ordering. These are imperative in the understanding of migrant behaviour. They enable an analysis of belongingness and an appreciation of the extent to which migrants are able to develop specific attachments towards foreign spaces.

Positioning and migration: rethinking strategic essentialism

Essentialising identities is part and parcel of the conscious and unconscious acceptance of specific elements of identity, especially for leverage. Most explanations of strategic essentialism situate the process in the contexts of group solidarity and group strategies. Different social groups are seen to situationally adopt specific standpoints that they use as a form of capital in different struggles. Strategic essentialism involves wearing identities and making them part of the arsenal of a group's strategies of dominance. One of the major aspects of understanding migration has been the idea of attempting to grasp struggles between two groups i.e. the hosts and the migrants. The seems to be an ever-present perception of competition for scarce resources between migrants and hosts. Whenever there are problems, shortages or negative occurrences, the easiest scapegoat becomes the migrant. Strategic essentialism allows an understanding of the behaviour portrayed by different groups in relation to their positioning within a context of resource allocation. The concept of strategic essentialism originated from Spivak's (1986) idea that individuals essentialise identities for different social and political purposes. Both migrant and host groups are seen to embrace certain stereotypes as they create impressions of victimhood in the process of migration. Strategic essentialism can help to understand a wide range of behaviour from migrants, officials, and hosts. It is a tool that brings greater clarity to the issues of belonging as it articulates how various groups strategically assume different ideas.

There is an apparent assumption of victimhood from the three groups of state, host communities and migrants. Migration is taken to be one of the major determinants of different kinds of political, social, and economic dynamics in South Africa. It is a campaigning point for political parties, a major factor in the social and moral decay, and a strain on the economic resources. This creates opportunities for the two host groups to essentialise migration thereby creating regimes of exclusion. For the politicians and officeholders, it is the reason why service delivery is poor, and it also accounts for their inability to deliver to the expectation of the citizens. There is an essentialisation of migration where the state appears to be inundated and overrun by migrants. This is reflected in the restrictive and defensive policy positions which seek to keep out migrant African foreigners or at least to reduce the rate at which they come into the country. There is also an established official phobia towards irregular African migrants and sometimes exaggeration of their role in the various socioeconomic crisis that the state takes pains to fix. For host communities, they have become the victims of migrants who occupy their spaces and outcompete them on the job market, as well as being responsible for creating social and moral crises as witnessed through criminal behaviour, drug trade and even intermarriages with locals. This creates a sense of victimhood among the host communities. The foreign African migrants themselves essentialise their vulnerability by claims of official neglect where they feel they are victimised by discriminatory state policies. They also appeal to issues of Africanity and ubuntu where they feel South Africa as a state has a responsibility for taking them in during their times of crises. Even formal migrants absorbed into the economy portray victimhood of discrimination and abuse due to their different foreign origins. It stands in the way of promotion, and results in numerous negative actions that they cannot challenge due to their foreignness. This shows a circulatory and situational assumption of victimhood by foreign African migrants as they seek to belong in South Africa.

Strategic essentialism should also be seen in terms of individual migrant strategies of coming to terms with the vagaries of adaptation in foreign spaces. It should be noted that even individuals can engage in essentialist behaviours. Strategic essentialism exploits the power of identity through using it as a tool for gaining an advantage in specific situations. In this situation, strategic essentialism can be equated to pragmatism (Spivak, 1996). It is characterised by the situational adoption of certain traits and identities in situations where the individual stands to benefit the most. To avoid the grand theorising tendencies of essentialisms, Spivak likens the usage of strategic essentialism to the discourse on deconstruction, arguing that although she sometimes uses deconstruction it does not denote that she becomes a deconstructivist (Eide, 2016). Hence the usage of strategic '...*can be read as pragmatic, since Spivak sees this essentialism as having little to do with theory, it rather defines a certain political practice*' (Eide, 2016, p. 1). Individual experiences of the migration process also benefit from strategic positioning. Migrants adopt different identities to gain access to resources and to help in their processes of integration into host communities. As discussed in Chapter five, some migrants mimic local cultures by appropriating their language, dress, and cultures so as to blend in with the local cultural groups. This gives them the access to those resources that most migrants fail to access.

Taking stock of migrant conflict: the frustration aggression theory

Migration often sparks conflicts with migrants as they are a group that is excluded and vulnerable. Conflicts and attacks on migrants have often been compartmentalised into discourses of xenophobia and Afrophobia. These discourses assume behavioural traits and intrinsic irrational fears of migrants by host communities. However, psychological theories of group behaviour may give better insights into the problems characterising contemporary struggles between migrants and host communities. As noted earlier, there is a tendency towards scapegoating and cloaking every ill in the country under the banner of migrants. They are the easier target whenever there is competition over resources. The frustration aggression model may further enlighten into the complexities surrounding migration and conflict. Rather than blanketing and labelling whole nations as xenophobic and Afrophobic (Paalo, Adu-Gyamfi and Arthur, 2022; Sibanda, 2022), there might be a need to contextualise the struggles and conflicts towards resources (Tewolde, 2020). It is argued that manifestations of conflict that are observed under the lenses of xenophobia and Afrophobia may indeed be evidence of struggles over resources and the limitations of the state to provide for its citizens. Conflicts affect the idea of belonging and give the migrants a perpetual label of outsiders. As will be seen in Chapter four, acquisition of citizenship often does not cure exclusionary actions towards foreign African migrants. Acceptance into South African communities is conditional, and differences always emerge whenever competition arises over resources. There is greater need to contextualise and conceptualise migration related conflicts in the light of competing interests over resources and the psychological tendency of communities to act in the interest of their perceived group membership. Exclusion is perpetual for migrants although its manifestation exists along a continuum. It is dormant in good situations, and erupts, sometimes violently, when the needs of individuals are blocked. This drives them to act in terms of their perceived rights and to attack objects that become associated with their inability to enjoy those rights.

Breakfast, Bradshaw and Nomarwayi (2019) note a direct correlation between violent conflict and lack of access to resources in South Africa. Writing on service delivery related conflicts, they note that both pre-and post-1994 eras in South Africa have been punctuated by episodes of violence as citizens protest against authorities. In migration politics this has been marked by sad episodes of mob killings of foreign African migrants and vigilantism that has been characteristic of citizenship disgruntlement towards what they perceive to be the official dereliction of duty towards curbing informal migration. A combination of psychological conceptions of relative deprivation and the frustration- aggression theory has often been put forward as an explanation for the behaviour of hosts towards migrants. Hence what others may conceptualise as politics of hate may be constructed in terms of local politico economic dynamics of distribution of resources as well as governance of migration.

A juxtaposition of the frustration aggression theory and strategic essentialism can also help to explain migrants hitting back at South Africa in terms of the obligations of the state towards their welfare. Some sectors of foreign African migrants hold South Africa responsible for their plight and even hold the state accountable for their presence in South Africa. This has been noted among Zimbabwean migrants who partially hold South Africa responsible for the political and economic crisis back in their country through the inability of the state to hold the Zimbabwean government accountable for several points of the country's governance crisis. They see the state as depriving them of better opportunities back home, hence their justification to have their rights of stay in South Africa. Other foreign African migrants unearth traditional historical cooperation and solidarity during colonial periods as instances where the needs of South Africa also affected their own development, hence the obligation of the South African state to accommodate them during their times of need. The relationship between people and resources is an important unit of analysis that can bring a greater understanding of the dynamics of citizenship and belonging. It results in people both assuming some standpoints as well as attacking those they feel are blocking their access to resources.

The ways in which state officials and politicians address issues of migration is also important in bringing out the interaction between strategic essentialism and relative deprivation. At times these policymakers attribute their failure to deliver services to a migration problem and they pose as victims of migration, simultaneously acquiring political capital by creating a rallying point of foreigners as increasing the competition over resources. This creates perceptions of deprivation with migrants being regarded as the source of resource scarcity.

Making Sense of Migration: Towards a unified theory

Migration flows continue to be a permanent feature of human societies. Increasing globalisation and the deepening inequalities across the world are likely to continue influencing global population flows. However, it remains important to try and understand the dynamics of citizenship and belonging to see how they are created and recreated over time. It calls for the development of theoretical lens to interpret migrant behaviour. Citizenship and belonging dynamics require multiple standpoints of interpreting and comprehending migration experiences. Citizenship can be approached from a standpoint of the movement control of individuals. In that situation, state mechanisms of defining the proper citizen and of shaping are witnessed as well as transforming the migrant into the proper 'citizen' mould. In this case, conceptualising the citizen is an ongoing and iterative process that incorporates not only stereotypical behaviour but also involves a progressive process of defining and redefining the citizen for migrants. Belonging in this case is a direct outcome of state actions, policies, attitudes, and behaviours towards migrants. The degree to which one's attachment to South Africa is manifested is an outcome of state attitudes of policymaking and control of the migrants.

The changes evident in the discourse of citizenship leads to the question of feasibility and the practicality of fully integrating into South African society. It raises the age-old questions of the possibility of changing one's identity and assuming another communal identity. Fredrick Barth's (2010) discussions on ethnicity shed light on the anthropological dynamics of inclusion and exclusion in different settings. Although he describes identity and belonging among ethnic groups, his observations resonate with how host communities and migrants are juxtaposed in relations of otherness. The migrant is a perpetual stranger and faces an insurmountable challenge to fully integrate into the host community. As discussed in Chapter four, there is a huge chasm between gaining legal status and becoming formally integrated into host communities. Most migrant lives remain islands, deriving their belongingness from their social networks which are mainly composed of other migrants who usually share similar roots. Looking at the South African case, there are Zimbabwean, Somali, Ethiopian, Nigerian and Congolese communities among others (Ojong 2005, Makanda 2016, Dekoke 2016, Akanle et al 2016). They have their own peculiar lifestyles, rituals and events that mark and perpetuate their difference in a foreign land. There is an evident boundary maintenance between migrants and host communities. Different acts of boundary maintenance reinforce the distinctions between the migrants and the hosts, sometimes resulting in regimes of inclusion and exclusion. Belonging hence becomes a struggle requiring answers to two questions. Firstly, to what extent do foreign migrants want to be immersed into host communities, and secondly how do host-migrant relations shape the feelings of belonging among migrants? The concept of *strangerness* is important in the articulation of the enduring otherization of the foreign African migrants. It enables an appreciation of difficulties of erasing the foreignnesss. Despite different dynamics of inclusion and integration into South African society, African others have carried stigmatized identities and their *strangerness* sometimes erupts whilst in other contexts it manifests in subtle ways. As noted by Ahmed (2000), *strangerness* is based on knowledge rather, than lack of it. It is constructed on definitions of home and those who belong and the simultaneous process of identifying those whom we might be familiar with but are regarded as out of place in our conceptualizations of home.

Given the enduring existence of difference, it is important to analyse how host-migrant interactions produce various elements including conflicts and specific attitudes towards each group. Elements of strategic essentialism enable the comprehension of situational assumptions of identity and portrayal of victimhood among hosts and migrants. Competition brings out the worst in either group, with perceptions towards access to resources creating tensions and mutual suspicions that prohibit bonding between migrants and host communities (Tarisayi and Manik, 2019). Psycho-anthropological conceptualisations of group behaviour enable the grasping of behaviours of different groups. A unified theory of migration should therefore bring out the complexity of migrant behaviour. It must articulate situational assumptions of identity and how these are situated in a broader context of migrant host relationships.

Conclusion

Belonging is a qualitative concept that tries to capture the degree of success in the community integration of outsiders. *Strangerness* seems to be unavoidable and it is an important way of understanding the host-immigrant interaction. Taking a top-down approach, *strangerness* is reinforced by official practices in law, policy making and law enforcement. These provide templates for whether the migrant can feel comfortable in South African society. The stringent conditions that African migrants must fulfil show the complexities of belongingness in the South African context. Moments of contestation and competition bring out the need to emphasise differences, something which becomes a perpetual reminder of the otherness of migrant African foreigners in South Africa.

This Chapter has explored the theoretical dynamics structuring the migration experiences. Control, resources, and positioning are seen to be important aspects of the migration experience. They influence the different dynamics of acceptability and belonging. Contemporary South African platforms for migration present a complex mixture of multiple factors that affect belonging. Although legal stay may be accessed, the complexities of daily interactions imply that the issue of identity and otherness will be the easier factors when it comes to issues of conflict. These ultimately shape the ability of migrant African foreigners to develop an attachment to place and belonging. The question of the possibility of an outsider becoming an insider thus remains. The following Chapter takes an historical approach to the understanding of the migration policymaking dynamics in South Africa.

Chapter 3

Review of Immigration Policies in South Africa: An Historical Perspective

Introduction

This Chapter addresses the policy movements and transformations towards migration. It examines the importance of policymaking in creating the milieu for the experience if citizenship and belonging. The question of who belongs and who should belong is explicitly set out in the policies. Both the written and unwritten aspects of policies create the environment for the experience of belonging. The Chapter begins by looking at the colonial policies that characterised the apartheid regime and proceeds to observe how the postcolonial South African government handled issues of citizenship, as well as the implications of belonging. To understand citizenship and belonging it is imperative to analyse the practices towards migrant Africans in the immigration policies of the state. Migration control, evident in instruments of exclusion such as borders and immigration policies, play a bigger role in the qualitative experience of belonging. By structuring how individual migrant legality is construed, these policies create perceptions and feelings toward belonging and in most instances may create feelings of transience among migrants. Historically, space and belonging have been seen to be situational, especially in Southern Africa, as most societies also depended on mobility as a key resource for their survival. Hence the colonial insistence on rigid borders and official control of movement has often been met by resistance and regimes of mobility that continue to undermine attempts to exclude foreign Africans. The continued mobility trends continue to be influenced by migration policies in a reciprocal manner.

Immigration Policy Prior to 1994 for Africans from other African Countries

The starting point of understanding migration in South Africa is to analyse the colonial population control mechanisms, especially the ways in which they structured the movement of foreign Africans into South Africa. Before 1994, South Africa immigration policies were structured to sustain the apartheid socio-economic and political systems. The two major pieces of legislation in apartheid South Africa were the 1913 Immigration Regulation Act and the 1991 Aliens Control Act which became the final instrument of population movement control by the apartheid government (Klotz, 2000). There is an evident racial bias in apartheid South African migrant policies with a relaxed attitude towards whites and an evident stifling of African migration. It has been observed that the policies were meant to protect the immigration of only white citizens and forestall the immigration of blacks, partly by creating a platform antagonistic to African needs and expectations, restricting their participation in the system to temporary engagement as cheap migrant labourers who could be returned to their places of origin after outliving their usefulness to the colonial economy (Amit and Kriger, 2014). In line with the absence of a liberal structure that could accommodate free movement of blacks, a major legislature to regulate immigration in the pre-democracy era was the Bantu Laws Amendment Act No. 76 of 1961. This Act made provision for the reception of migrants from certain countries but placed stringent measures on the inflow of migrants from African countries, mainly Botswana, Lesotho, Malawi, Mozambique, Swaziland, then designated as 'peripheral labour reserves' (Tati, 2015). Through this Act, the immigration policy was partly meant to create an intimidating platform to ensure the steady supply of cheap labour from the 'peripheral labour reserves' for the South African mining industry, particularly the gold and diamonds fields, as well as from agriculture.

The tenet of this Act restricted labour migrants from the 'peripheral labour reserves' to jobs in the mining industry and agriculture. It placed serious restriction on migrants from the aforementioned states who were not interested in the mining and agricultural sector. It is observed that "on the South Africa side, the same legislation made it mandatory for employers hiring foreign Africans from Swaziland, Botswana and Lesotho to undertake their repatriation upon expiration of contract" (Tati, 2015:429). What should be underscored is the observation that the migration of Africans was always characterised by impermanence. There was little or no room for the recognition of

African immigration (Amit and Kriger, 2014).

The migration policies of the apartheid regime also encompassed a host of other issues. These included the establishment of the border management authority and designation of point of entry (POE). The Customs and Excise Act of 1964 (Act No 91 of 1964) was enacted to address issues in this category and to regulate the decisions and activities of the commissioner in charge (DHA, 2017). The Act was considered significant, particularly in the operation of "some of the maritime ports where there are various terminals and at some… POE where passenger segmentation is applied, e.g. pedestrians, truck drivers, etc." and for creating a platform that can ensure "the establishment of rail ports of entry where goods and passengers may be inspected in accordance with the business processes applicable in other POE" (DHA, 2017:37). Also related are the International Health Regulations of 1974 (Act No 28 of 1974) which was meant to designate places that may serve as ports of entry. Therefore, its provisions were meant to manage this aspect of the immigration system, including the need for new strategies and logistics in relation to emerging challenges and projection into the future. It can be noted that the monitoring of the movement of people through establishing official points of entry disrupted existing cross-border community relationships by keeping Africans along rigid spaces according to the colonial demarcation of states (Macdonald, 2012).

The Immigration Policy of the Post-Apartheid State

Klotz (2000) argues that in practice, South African immigration policy from 1994 to 2000 was largely a continuation of the trend and set-down pattern created since the 1913 Immigration Regulation Act. Thus, he observed a trend of continuity, but one sustained with little or no dynamism. The author is of the view that despite the enactment of new immigration laws since the commencement of democracy in 1994, "the government actively sought white settlers but strictly limited Africans to no more than temporary legal entry under the migrant labour system throughout the twentieth century (Klotz, 2000:830). Maunganidze (2021), Tati (2015), Amit and Kriger (2014), and Belvedere (2008) are also of the view that the immigration policies of the democratic regime have placed enormous limitations on the demands and human rights benefits of African immigrants simply because the system has been structurally polarised by the xenophobic social institution, thus considerably reducing the expected level of dynamism. The bottom line is that the immigration policies of apartheid were framed to uphold white immigration and side-line and reduce the inflow of African migrants while those of the democracy era were polarized by the rapidly evolving xenophobic culture meant solely to forestall the immigration of blacks from neighbouring African countries but with a neutral position on the immigration interests of whites. This is why, in its assessment of the immigration policy trend up to 2000, Klotz (2000:832) concludes that "in sum, not much has changed since the 1913 Immigration Regulation Act."

Summarising the continuity, Tati (2015:429) states that "xenophobia in South Africa is a direct effect of a particular kind of politics, a particular kind of state which was forged in opposition to the manner in which the apartheid state interpellated its subjects" and that "in the post-apartheid state, politicians and state institutions have their parts in the making of a culture of xenophobia, and this has filtered down to the whole of society." The analyses of these studies tend to support the claim that in both the apartheid and democratic regime, some African migrants might have served as the scapegoats and pariahs while some were engaged as the guinea pigs where there was need for experiment, e.g., in the mines of the apartheid regime, and assignments considered too odd for natives in the post-apartheid era.

The 1961 Act was created for the purpose of alien control and was supported in 1974 by the policy of internalisation. They were among the pivoting instruments of the apartheid immigration policy. These sustained the policy framework until the immigration laws of the 1980s and 1990s which had some of their provisions retained in the post-apartheid government. Thus there was a major immigration law in 1981 later followed by the Refugee Act 130 of 1988. This Act was adopted to bring into reality South Africa's undertakings regarding the management of refugee as contained in the 1951 United Nations Refugee Convention and a similar agreement with the Organization of Africa Unity (OAU) in 1969. The next was the Aliens Control Act of 1991 which was retained by the post-apartheid regime and was among the instruments employed to sustain continuity in the immigration policy. Its terms were such that it is regarded by some critics as "possibly the ugliest leftover from apartheid still on the statute books" (Tessier, 1995:257). In this respect, Moyo (2021:8) also observes that "The Aliens Control Act of 1991 was at odds with the new democratic dispensation and yet remained in place for several years after the arrival of democracy and was responsible for hundreds of thousands of arrests and deportations annually."

Therefore the government of the African National Congress (ANC) could be said to have been faced with a political dilemma in its effort to reconcile the xenophobic anti-immigrant posture of its African citizens with the immigration demands of neighbouring African states who offered relentless support to South African blacks against the defunct white minority regime (Tessier, 1995). In trying to strike a balance, some of the key political figures in policy formulation had it wrong as over 50000 immigrants of Mozambican origin were deported within a period of just two months in 1994 (Tessier, 1995). One of such personalities was Chief Mangosuthu Buthelezi, the Minister of Home Affairs, formerly the leader of a political group, the Inkatha Freedom Party. As the central figure in the formulation of immigration policies for the government and at the same time a key exponent of the anti-immigration policy, with particular focus on African migrants, the immigration laws became subjective and tended to be biased against African immigrants from neighbouring countries (Tessier, 1995). In fact, it was the white academics and professionals that supported a liberal immigration policy in favour of all races including blacks during a conference held on the issue after the inauguration of a democratic government. Their black counterparts including black academics completely rejected this and insisted on the implementation of a system with stringent restrictions on the inflow of black migrants from other African countries (Tessier, 1995). This is why a number of studies perceive xenophobia as a culture supported by the state through its institutions and politicians and was allowed to penetrate the social fabrics of the society as a means of sustaining the above immigration policy (Tati, 2015; Belvedere, 2008).

But if the viewpoints of the above authors capture the immigration trend up to 2000, can these also empirically explain the immigration policy focus since 2001? Looking at this question, Moyo (2021) identifies some features of the policy trend up to 2000 in the new era which could be said to have commenced with the Immigration

Act of 2002. According to the author, although the Immigration Act of 2002 replaced the Alien Control Act of 1991 and sought to prevent irregular migration, it was still clouded with traces of the apartheid legislature with provisions that completely side-lined some category of migrants while granting access to others, even after its amendment in 2007 and 2011. Therefore, in his assessment of the immigration policy up to the present decade, the author contends that despite the end to racial restriction of black South Africans in the post-apartheid era, there is "no clean break in policy" focus as far as immigration is concerned". Sawa (2016:26) has a similar view based on the Immigration Act 13 of 2002 as amended in 2014. The author argues that "despite recommendation to the government to relax its immigration laws, the 2014 amendment of the Immigration Act rather increased the barrier to migration to all categories of migrants." In this context it is important to note that four years later, another immigration law otherwise known as the 2018 Immigration Act Amendment Bill specifically included clauses for the detention of 'illegal foreigners' and this was structured for further scrutiny of affected immigrants to gather enough evidence that can justify their deportation (Maunganidze, 2021). The general consensus seems to support the opinion that the state is not doing enough to address the challenges of South Africa immigration policies.

One viewpoint published by the Centre for Development and Enterprise (CDE) of South Africa, however, is that "migration is a process that governments learn to manage, it is not a problem that governments ever solve" (Martin, 2011:9). Articles in this volume compiled from a workshop sponsored by CDE in 2011 try to highlight the effort made so far by the government to minimize what Tessier (1995:258) referred to as South Africa's "hard-line position on immigration." Among these is an improvement in border control (Maphosa, 2011) and efforts to minimise the requirements for the acquisition of visas by migrants from some neighbouring states, particularly Zimbabwe (Makina, 2011). However, they admit that previous challenges in South Africa's migration system and the search for a way forward were poorly managed and that the need for a "new approach to South African migration policy and its implementation is long overdue" (CDE, 2011:7). Among the challenges admitted to be poorly managed is the handling of migrants from neighbouring

African states. Others are the management of porous borders and the adoption of appropriate parameters to define the interests of South Africans vis-à-vis the inflow of migrants.

Citizenship Status

Migration has also been a key issue in analysing citizenship status and its legal paraphernalia in South Africa (Bilchitz & Ziegler, 2023; Tati, 2015; Klaaren, 2008; Belvedere, 2008; Neocosmos, 2006). The immigration law recognises citizenship by naturalisation and descent apart from the popular citizenship by birth based on the South Africa Citizenship Act (SACA). However, the amendment of the citizenship laws since 2010 (Amendment Act: No. 17 of 2010) has attracted some criticisms. By this amendment, children born to some categories of non-citizens in South Africa cannot be granted citizenship status until they reach the age of majority (Hobden, 2018). Overall, there have been elements of continuity as some of the tenets and principles adopted by SACA itself, particularly with regard to gender issues, have been in operation since before the democratic government. From a perspective of the legal system, it has been argued that SACA "did not make far-reaching substantive changes to the pre-existing South African rules of citizenship—except in the significant aspect that it made citizenship rules uniform through the Republic" (Klaaren, 2000:221).

Nevertheless, there have been a number of changes introduced by the current regime, partly under the platform of SACA, among which is the removal of cumbersome processes endorsed by the apartheid regime including undue emphasis on the gender of parents with regard to recognition of the child citizenship. SACA itself did not result from the amendment of the apartheid citizenship immigration laws, but was created in 1995 to replace them (Hobden, 2018). Therefore, it came up with a number of ideas to improve on the existing citizenship laws, a step that also led to the constitutional approval of citizenship by birth for the stateless child in 2010 (Klaaren, 2010:223). This refers to citizenship granted to a child born in South Africa and registered according to the Birth and Death Registration Act (BDRA) but "has no citizenship or nationality of another country and has no right to such citizenship or nationality" (Hobden, 2018:10). In the case of naturalisation, it has been observed that it is largely based on the structure created by the apartheid government, and this has been the trend since 1994. But the 2010 Amendment Act introduced a change stating that one who acquires South Africa citizenship through naturalisation automatically loses it if he/she engages "in a war that the country does not support under the flag of another country" (Hobden, 2018:10).

Some key changes have also been introduced with regard to individuals seeking naturalisation through marriage (Kavuro, 2021). In 2003, an immigration law was introduced that rejected marriages of convenience even though the term 'marriage of convenience' is not clearly defined in South Africa's legislature. In the South African context, the immigration policy since 2003 and also reflected in the 2021 Green Paper on Marriages in South Africa, regards a marriage of convenience as one contracted "for monetary gain and for obtaining a legal residence in the country" (Kavuro, 2021:525). But the legislative lapses in the definition of the concept has generated serious legal complications in its application even resulting in legal actions against the government by couples facing such allegations (Kavuro, 2021:525 & 536). Another immigration law facing similar legal complication is the Citizenship Act 68 of 1995 which "stipulates that adult citizens automatically lose their South African citizenship when they 'freely and voluntarily' acquire another citizenship (except through marriage) without first applying for and obtaining a ministerial certificate authorizing this" Bilchitz & Ziegler (2023:5).

Property ownership and investment constitutes an asset for immigrants seeking a permanent residence permit (PRP) or citizenship through naturalisation. It is claimed that the current immigration policy approved by the Department of Home Affairs (DHA) may place more emphasis on this than the duration of time the immigrant has spent in the country (Malope, 2019). However, this can be categorised as a recent development since according to existing data, none of the permanent residence permits (PRPs) recorded by the DHA between 2014 and 2016 was based primarily on property ownership. Of the 46,100 PRPs granted during the period "the highest percentage was issued to spouses (35%), workers (18%) and persons with extraordinary skills (9%)", while refugees had 4% (Handmaker & Nalule, 2021:19). Although the source could not explain the determinant of the remaining 36%, it is silent on the issue of property ownership. Even if property ownership counts in this regard, it is clear that the DHA has started placing stringent restrictions on citizenship acquisition since 2020 (Handmaker & Nalule, 2021; Kavuro, 2021).

Legal requirements for citizenship also incorporate gender issues (Hobden, 2018). In the aspect of gender equality, the democratic government has improved tremendously on that which was inherited from apartheid regime (Hobden, 2018). The immigration policy of the new government replaced loyalty to customs and tradition with that of gender equality. This policy was partly influenced by the policy focus of the ANC where women constitute 50% of all key committees. However, it derived more influence from the dynamics and new trends in the global feminist movement (Hobden, 2018).

Entrepreneurship and Business Ownership

Migration policies involving entrepreneurship and business enterprises might not have addressed the human rights expectations of most immigrants in this sector, as many migrants complain about a biased socio-economic platform that labels them as individuals in the country to compete with and acquire what belong to indigenes (Ojong, et al., 2018). But there was an enabling social terrain for them to embark on a number of business ventures, including small-scale business outfits. For instance, the taxation policy does not tax small-scale enterprises and this enables them to reduce costs, making their services and products easily affordable to the poor (Sawa, 2016). Yet these enterprises contribute enormously to the state revenue in addition to employing a number of South Africans, particularly the low-skilled young ones, while giving some the opportunity to acquire "practical entrepreneurial skills and artisanal knowledge to enable them start their own business" (Sawa, 2016:48). Many of those in small-scale businesses have been able to identify a niche that they exploit to make enough profit and even employ South Africans.

But the regulating immigration policies for managing these immigrants in the informal sector of the economy have been faulted in one way or the other (Siddique, 2005). The major one is the Aliens Control Act of 1991 inherited by the democratic government in

1994, but amended in 1995, to enable it respond to changes in the system in terms of new socio-economic trends and national interests. According to Siddique (2005) and Peberdy (1997), its many restrictions were counter-productive to these sets of entrepreneurs. At the same time, its management is considered cumbersome as traders were frequently reapplying for visas because only a single entry was issued at a time. This is said to have created a bureaucratic structure for the exploitation of these traders by the staff of the DHA, and Customs and Excise as well as the police, until its replacement by a bill practical enough to issue visas in the form of temporary permits that grant traders multiple entries without any form of ambiguity (Siddique, 2005).

In addition, a new element was added to the immigration policy at the peak of the COVID-19 era. The law for the closure of shops only affects immigrants or was at least applied more strictly to them than citizens. In most places, immigrants were only allowed to open their business outfits when it was found that this would be beneficial to indigenes by enabling them to get what they needed, particularly food, without walking long distances (Moyo, 2020).

Beyond the small-scale businesses, the analysis of the current immigration policies reveals that foreigners are not issued with work permits until there is enough evidence to confirm that the number of South Africans skilled for such jobs are insufficient, or for one reason or the other indigenes may not be interested in such jobs (Siddique, 2005:10; Crush, 1997:3-4). However, amnesty has been employed since 1994 through the immigration policy to assist certain categories of immigrants in the search for a source of income. The government announced the first amnesty in 1995 and it was employed to assist immigrant workers in the mines to acquire permanent residence. The beneficiaries were those who have worked in the mines for a minimum of ten years with evidence of participation in the 1994 national elections (Crush, 1997:6).

Refugees and Asylum

Policies involving the management of refugees and asylum seekers were believed to be accommodating as from 1994 following the adoption of democratic principles. It has been observed that "the

Refugees Act of 1998 allows asylum seekers to move freely, work, and study in the country during the lengthy adjudication process" (Moyo, 2021). This was the trend until 2000. Thereafter, the government found that the liberal principles of the 1998 Act were being abused, citing evidence of people who hide under the canopy of such principles to achieve their selfish interests at expense of the law. This led to the amendments of 2008, 2011, and 2017 to align with the new laws structured to monitor asylum seekers and those meant to identify and handle irregularities in the system with regard to the total figures of refugees and asylum seekers, including parameters for determining their inflow.

It has been observed that currently there are a host of issues that make South Africa's refugee and asylum system difficult to access (Carmel, 2015). Apart from the nature of the waiting time which is considered long, decision making guiding the processing and final approval tends to be patchy in number of ways (Maunganidze, 2021). There is accumulation of applications with regard to refugee and asylum seekers arising from the fact that applicants wait for a long time. The situation has been criticised by a number of analysts and human rights lawyers. This has attracted a host of litigations, e.g. over 1,200 immigration cases against the DHA between 2016 and 2017 in addition to 1,900 asylum litigations within the same period.

There have been steps in the DHA to come up with policies that can reduce the number of applications for asylum and the body seems to perceive that this can be achieved by reducing anything that tends to serve as an incentive to asylum seekers in addition to placing any possible restrictions. Identifying and correcting the lapses in the DHA processing system would be helpful in the search for the right policy focus (Maunganidze, 2021). In practice, the DHA seems to be one-sided by overemphasising the high rate of asylum seekers interested in the country. In 2017, the idea of processing centres was conceived following the White Paper issued by the government in the same year. The processing centres were meant to host asylum seekers, while the processing of their documents is yet to be finalised. The building of these centres was expensive as it cost R290 million to build one. The human rights cost was equally expensive and yet it is observed that these centres "mirror detention facilities in everything but name" (Maunganidze, 2021:15).

The DHA attitude is largely dictated by an emerging belief that the asylum and refugee system is being abused by a set of migration aspirants, particularly economic migrants, who enter the country through the asylum package and exploit it for other purposes. As a result of this, there were a host of other barriers employed to restrict asylum seekers. One of them is the nature of fines arbitrarily introduced after the expiriy date for renewal. This varies in amount, "but are often prohibitively expensive, making it impossible for an individual to renew his or her permit" and "individuals who lose their permits (or have them stolen) face similar difficulties and may be unable to pay the fine" (Amit and Kriger, 2014:280).

Late renewals may arise from illness, distant residence from the office, long queues in the process, restrictions placed by the place of work with regard to permission to be absent for such issues and the likes. This is also compounded for individuals by the custom of compelling them to do the renewal in the Refugee Reception Office (RRO) where they were originally registered. In most cases such an office is far away and sometimes located at the border (Amit and Kriger, 2014). Yet most asylum seekers support themselves financially as they receive little or no social support. The implication of this in terms of logistics and finance is that when the affected individuals are unable to renew their permit in the original office of registration, they may get arrested in the process of trying to locate one in the urban centres. In addition, in 2013 the DHA introduced a policy that does not allow a permit to be renewed more than 12 times, even though in most cases the need for continued renewal was created by inefficiencies emanating from the bureaucracy of the body (Amit and Kriger, 2014). This has been the trend up till the beginning of this decade, despite the expectation of improvement through an annual or occasional policy review of the immigration sector (Maunganidze, 2021; Bilchitz & Ziegler, 2023). Overall, legislation is rather devising the means "to decrease the attractiveness of applying for asylum in South Africa" in addition to a removal of the "automatic right for asylum seekers to work, study, or conduct business" based on the "2017 Amendment of the Refugee Act" which is still in operation (Maunganidze, 2021:15).

Therefore, from an assessment of the overall immigration policy framework including a clear consideration of the legal issues surrounding citizenship, entrepreneurship and business ownership as well as asylum and refugees, there are changes and continuity in the policy trend. But what is the overall impact of this on the society in terms of national development and benefits to the individual South African citizen, at least those directly or indirectly involved in immigration in one way or the other? In the light of the existing facts and figures, a major credit to the immigration policy of the post-apartheid government is the operation of a uniform legal system that responds to the human rights viewpoints of all indigenous racial groups including those in support of institutionalising xenophobia as a social system. But beyond this, there is still much room for improvement with regard to the human rights demands of immigrants. In this case, the overall scene based on existing data and analyses tend to indicate that the plight of African immigrants needs to be given some consideration (Maunganidze, 2021). It is also the need to have a second look at the drawing board in order to improve on the country's immigration policy focus that made the International Business News (IBN, 2020) write:

> "South Africa has not yet built consensus on how to manage international migration for development. There is a lack of a holistic and whole-of-government-and-society approach. The existing policy is based on an approach that is largely static and is limited to compliance rather than to managing international migration strategically to achieve national goals. In addition, there is no sense of South Africa being an African state situated in the SADC, which is one of the eight regional communities recognised by the African Union (AU)". (IBN, 2020: 3)

Conclusion

The South African immigration policies before the transition into democracy were structured to serve the socio-economic interests of the apartheid regime that ignored the wellbeing of the majority. This was reflected in the laws of the regime, including the 1981 Immigration Law later followed by the Refugee Act 130 of 1988 and even the Aliens Control Act of 1991. The democratic government inaugurated in 1994 was expected to review the entire system and come up with immigration policies that accommodate the interests of all stakeholders. The stakeholders in this context include the government and citizens of South Africa upon a platform that incorporates the views and expectations of the various races and sub-groups in the country. They also include migrants from different African countries and other regions of the world. The democratic government came up with new immigration laws with the conscious effort of fashioning its own policy as reflected in various laws, up to current acts like the 2018 Immigration Act Amendment Bill.

Yet there is a perception among a number of authors and analysts that the immigration policy of the current democratic government is largely a continuation of the trend inherited from the apartheid regime (Tessier, 1995; Klotz, 2000; Amit and Kriger, 2014; Tati, 2015; Moyo, 2021). This arises from the fact that the formulation and implementation of immigration laws of the current regime were polarised and sometimes rubbished by institutionalised xenophobia just as those of the pre-democracy government were implemented to address the institutional interests of apartheid as a social system. In other words, a summary of their viewpoints is that most of the previous immigration laws have been discarded and replaced with new ones, but this has not yielded the expected level of transformation and dynamism in policy focus. Thus, as Klotz (2000:831) simply puts it "a new non-racial xenophobia creates a potent barrier to reform." This is reflected in the management of the immigration legal system with regard to the acquisition of citizenship, immigrant entrepreneurship, asylum and refugee systems and marriage laws under immigration.

It must be admitted that the government was faced with a herculean task in respect of immigration. For one thing, economic disparity is the primary reason for the influx of immigrants from other African countries, particularly the SADC region, into South Africa. Although the population of South Africa is about one-third of that of the entire SADC region, its Gross Domestic Product (GDP) is over three times that of all other states put together (Siddique, 2005). The state was trapped between two sets of stakeholders, namely the migration aspirants from neighbouring African countries which offered relentless support to the black freedom fighters in South Africa during the apartheid regime, and the South African blacks who perceived the arrival of immigrants as a threat to their economic interests. It is an intricate scene that needed to be approached with well-conceived principles and policy focus, but as explained above, some of the key political figures in policy formulation were wrong.

Nevertheless, the immigration policy of the democratic government since 1994 is not without some façade of dynamism and an element of improvement upon what it inherited from the apartheid era (Sawa, 2016; Martin, 2011; Siddique, 2005). In the first place, it has been able to accommodate the interests of all races in the country, compared to the apartheid regime whose immigration policy was structured to only address the demands of the white minority race. Thus, as Siddique (2005:11) puts it, "in this case, the political decision-making process appears to be reflecting popular views." It has also effectively responded to key demands of blacks of South African origin, although this is sometimes at the expense of the human rights expectations of immigrants from other African countries.

The next chapters attempt to capture the continued otherization of foreign African migrants in South Africa. Whilst it has been noted that the needs of South Africans are converging and attempts have been made to redress historical discrimination, the same can not be said of foreign African migrants who appear to be on the blind side of the discourses of inclusion. In the next chapter, we focus on the legal system and policymaking framework to understand how it has shaped the belonging of the African others.

Chapter 4

Navigating Contemporary Citizenship. Legality and Belonging

Introduction

The experiential dynamics of citizenship are best understood by the contracts between migrants and the legal aspects that they must fulfil to be considered legal individuals in South Africa. This Chapter examines the struggles of the African migrants for citizenship in contemporary South Africa. The previous Chapter examined how historical processes shaped the legal requirements of belonging and this Chapter documents the contemporary experiences of African migrants who seek to obtain legal status in the country. The various experiences of individuals from mostly African countries are explored, showing how their interactions with the legal institutions regulating migration have shaped their experiences in South Africa. The previous Chapter also showed the limited avenues of naturalisation in South Africa, characterised by permanent residence, birth and marriage. These are the three popular legal contexts that lead to the acquisition of citizenship (Sadiq, 2008; Muzondidya, 2010). However, there is an overwhelming presence of long-term African migrants in the country. One of the mechanisms that have been used has been the issue of seeking refuge in the country (Klaaren, 2000). The legal classification of migrants is important as a mechanism that allows understanding the creation of belonging. African migrants have inhabited the South African space through legal visa applications, and illegal entry through formal and informal methods (Handmaker and Parsley, 2001; Landau, 2011; Moyo and Zanker, 2020). There has been an influx of migrants who utilised the political asylum and refugee method to navigate the legal issues of staying in South Africa.

Citizenship and legal residence in South Africa have not been the same for all migrant Africans. There has been a differential treatment of African migrants with different groups receiving context specific treatment. It is argued that there is a general lack of a standardised approach to legal status in South Africa, and this has created varied experiences among foreign migrant Africans. Some of the legal instruments shaping migrants legal stay include the Zimbabwe Exemption Permit, and the Lesotho Pass. The Chapter also links contemporary experiences to historical migration approaches so as to explore continuities and discontinuities characterising citizenship experiences. The Chapter also makes use of ethnographic experiences to document the narratives of foreign African migrants and their experiences in legalising their stay in South Africa.

Legalising regimes produce inclusion and exclusion based on labels associated with the identities that stem out of the legalising, process. Migrants fall into two categories, the legal and the illegal, based on official discourses governing migration. Legality is the first step towards the naturalisation and acquisition of legal citizenship. The state, through formal and informal means, controls this process and attempts to direct the migration trends to include some whilst others are kept out of the system. Hence the first aspect discussed in this Chapter is the making and unmaking of the citizen, where the ways of legalisation and illegalisation of migrants are explored. Moreover, it can be argued that the South African state is hesitant about allowing the naturalisation of migrants, therefore most of the state processes have been responsible for keeping migrants in a perpetual state of temporariness, denying them the opportunity to progress through to become South African citizens. The process of naturalisation is too narrow and keeps most migrants outside the system. In the following section the dual processes of making and unmaking of the African migrant through the legal system are explored. The Chapter also explores the stratagems employed by foreign African migrants to respond to the constrictions of the space for legality and citizenship in South Africa.

The (un)making of the migrant citizen

Contemporary South Africa is inward looking. Although African migrants continue to bombard the South African state, there is a complex rebuttal and tightening of processes that enable one to acquire citizenship in South Africa. There is a general anti-migrant sentiment canonized and cloaked in official law and policymaking.

The making and unmaking of the citizen can be seen through official and unofficial strategies that either promote or constrict the path towards the attainment of citizenship. Although there are laid out procedures for acquiring citizenship, there are different strategies that reduce migrant eligibility to naturalise and to take advantage of existing legislations. The situation is more complex for African migrants who do not possess skills that the country require. However, the situation is increasingly becoming difficult even for skilled African migrants. There has been an evident shifting of requirements as well as both written and unwritten rules of tightening the migration process. Using the lens of skilled migrants, this section shows that possession of requisite skills is no longer a guarantee for ensuring that their stay in South Africa will be straightforward. Narratives from various respondents in professional circles showed the numerous challenges that they face in terms of the legal pursuit of residence in South Africa. The instrument of permanent residence is one that has also been used as a way of ensuring that those with critical skills are welcomed into the South African economy. As noted earlier, critical skills afforded migrant workers sufficient leeway to be legal residents and to work unencumbered for at least five years. It was also an easier route to gaining a permanent residence permit. However, recent developments show that the process has been tightened, with individuals being given yearly renewals subject to evidence of employment in South Africa. The life of the migrant citizen is characterized by a legal precarity where access to legal avenues of citizenship is becoming increasingly difficult.

There is a dual process of making and unmaking where on one hand the State is creating avenues for the attainment of citizenship whilst there is a simultaneous process of reversing the process and tightening the requirements for gaining legal citizenship. The qualitative part of belonging is highly dependent on individuals' experiences of formality and informality. As migrants experience systemic discrimination, their feelings and attachment to place is transformed. One tool through which the unmaking of citizens is occurring is through the tool of waiting. The periods taken for one to get a decision over their applications is increasing in a manner that keeps the migrant in a mode of temporariness. The DHA has been complaining of being understaffed and failing to cope with large applications. The ever-changing bureaucratic procedures also compounds the situation as there is an official desire to close loopholes that may allow the legalisation of undeserving migrants. This has created a discourse of waiting, characterised by migrants being kept in a perpetual temporary mode.

Citizenship has been shown to be based on several things. These include the legality of residence and recognition of the length of stay. However, there are ever-changing dynamics that create hurdles in the access to citizenship in South Africa.The making and unmaking of citizens stem from practices that cement the salience of the other. The discourse of the real South African against the other is growing and influencing the undermining of foreign African migrants' claim to belonging in South Africa. The unmaking has had a much higher impact on the legal migrants as shown from the narrative of one migrant named Jason. He came to South Africa in 2010 and managed to go through the academic route. He completed his master's and doctoral degrees in the country and after completion he applied for a critical skills visa and subsequently a permanent residence permit. These documents enabled him to have the required legality in the country and put him on the path of being granted citizenship. After more than 10 years in the country, Jason managed to acquire some limited linguistic skills that allowed him to have conversation and interact with the locals. During interviews he noted that whenever the locals see another black person, their normal reaction and assumption is that you must be able to comprehend and have conversation in some of the local languages, hence it is a good skill to learn few local languages.

There is evidence of a hidden presence of African migrants. Some migrants end up living 'under the radar' of official interaction as they try to avoid the spotlight that can affect their presence in South Africa. These hidden lives of migrants are survival strategies meant to ensure that they avoid situations that call their identity into question, thereby triggering negative attitudes based on their foreignness. The invisibility shields the African migrant from scrutiny and possible repercussions of being labelled an outsider. There is evidence of official and unofficial strategies at unmaking the citizenship of African migrants. This is demonstrated in official dual policies of documentation and silence towards migrants. Post-

COVID 19 South Africa has experienced heightened attempts at the unmaking of African citizenship. This can be traced through processes of cumbersome documentation procedures, complex and unreasonable demands towards migrants, and seemingly deliberate bureaucratic delays in processing the legal documents of the migrants. Respondents noted that it was increasingly difficult to get decisions from the DHA and sometimes they would be granted late. One postdoctoral fellow worked online whilst awaiting his visa application decision. He worked for more than a year without getting paid due to the absence of legal documentation to facilitate the release of funds. Some respondents also pointed to lost opportunities where organisations would simply withdraw offers to foreign Africans due to the complexities surrounding the granting of legal documents. The DHA is continuing a path of bureaucratic ambivalence, characterised on one hand by efforts at increasing documentation and knowledge of foreign nationals, whist on the other hand, there is an almost deliberate attempt at illegalising migrant foreigners through complicating documentation processes and delaying making decisions on visa applications (Amit and Kriger, 2014). The unmaking process reflects the evidence of official prejudice against migration processes. It comes from undermining and understating the contributions of the African foreigners to the South African socioeconomic landscape. Evidence of slowness by both potential African applicants and South African organisations reflect the effects of the official handling of the migration processes. It is increasingly difficult for African migrants to get opportunities as both the process of hiring and cost of getting official documentation are becoming increasingly difficult.

The unmaking process can be seen to proceed from bottlenecks at the point of entry. As shown previously, restricting the eligibility of foreigners is one strategy used by the state to control the migration process. On the other hand, practices towards those already in the system are stimulating migrant explorations of possible alternative migration destinations. Acquiring a temporary residence visa is a step that allows migrants to enter the system and to start working towards permanent residence and ultimately achieve full naturalisation through gaining South African citizenship. The process is arduous, requiring testimonials, recommendations and evidence of the positive contribution and integration into the South African society. As one respondent noted, he had to get recommendations from work, and show an appreciation of local connections through establishing relationships with locals who could testify and support his application for citizenship. There is also an inherent stratification among the migrants, with those in formal well-paying jobs finding it relatively easy to navigate the terrain of citizenship. They also face limited overt resistance and alienation since most of the times their work, residence and communities are more elitist, creating a significant barrier to the conflicts that lower class migrants encounter daily.

Whilst problems of citizenship are often thought to affect irregular migrants who are characterised by low skills and lower educational levels, the unmaking process has affected even highly skilled and qualified personnel. Although the policy thrust of restricting immigration has been noted to affect mostly lower class and unskilled migrants, experiences by highly skilled migrants reflect an indiscriminate anti migrant sentiment. One group that had the privilege of higher chances for access to documentation and permits has been the academic group. Academia has been part of another professional avenue through which African migrants acquire citizenship in South Africa. It has allowed the entry of skilled personnel and retention of skills in South African universities. Upon attaining the requisite skills, most individuals have been able to apply for a critical skills visa which has been an avenue towards the acquisition of a permanent residence permit. However, the sphere has not escaped the changing requirements and tightening of the legal status acquisition in South Africa.

The issues of migrant classification also affect their citizenship status in South Africa. There has been a tendency to create categories of definition for migrants that has a net effect of determining their access to South Africa. As noted earlier, civil citizenship can be acquired through acquiring documentation such as permanent residence and the subsequent naturalisation of the migrant. Before getting to such procedures, the ways in which the migrant's presence on South African soil has implications for their ability to acquire permanence. The designation of most African migrants as economic migrants has the effect of blocking the space for further acquiring citizenship, either through the period of stay or other bases. It imprisons the migrant into a perpetual position of being a temporary resident without the possibility of ever officially transforming their stay into the recognized categories. This creates increasingly difficult conditions for the migrant to establish roots and cultivate feelings of belonging in South Africa. One of the respondents who has been in South Africa for the past ten years noted that he was hesitant to bring his family over to South Africa as he was never sure of when he could continue to be in the country. He noted the difficulties involved in relocating the whole family into a 'temporary' space. Despite the notable length of stay, the migrant still felt feelings of transience and temporariness. He remains in a waiting mode, waiting for things to be better so that he can bring over his family.

The unmaking process is also influenced by the daily practices of settled migrants as they try to adapt to the present circumstances in the South African spaces. There are various hindrances to full integration and attempts at closing the space for the possibility of full citizenship for African migrants. These usually stem from the legal perspectives that structure the conditions of existence of the migrants. Changing legal designations have implications on how people's relationship to space is constructed and constituted. The following sections explore the experiences of individuals under the Zimbabwe Exemption Permits (ZEP) and how their perceptions and experiences have been affected by continuous redefinition of their identity and status in South Africa. There is also a comparison made with the Lesotho Pass. These groups have experienced considerable access to South Africa, due to policies enabling their temporary residence and access to the labour market in South Africa. The SADC-based three months temporary visas that are awarded and how they have been instrumental in negotiating legality in South Africa are also discussed.

Always in Limbo: Uncertain Futures of Zimbabwean Special Permits

Zimbabwean movement into South Africa has often been characterised by circular migration as various people oscillated between Zimbabwe and South Africa (Crush et al., 2012). Short periodic stays for employment and trade constituted the major migration trends. Even those who had longer term employment maintained strong ties with their Zimbabwean families and would frequently travel between the two countries. However, deepening poverty and instability in Zimbabwe influenced new trends in the migration process, with evidence of permanent settlement being on the cards for new migrants. Crush et al. (2012) note an increase in Zimbabwean migrants who did not frequently return home as compared to previous migration trends. Pegged at 46% it is undeniable that the proportion of Zimbabweans choosing to stay indefinitely in South Africa is growing. Moreover, the decrease in visiting Zimbabwe points to a reduction in family obligations implying that most of the migrants are bringing their immediate families into South Africa.

The political and economic crisis in Zimbabwe caused a considerable number of people to move to South Africa, creating an influx of Zimbabweans in the country. In a bid to deal with the dynamics of the situation, the state came up with the Zimbabwean Documentation Programme (ZDP) that allowed holders permission to stay, study, engage in business, and to look for employment. The programme was meant to provide solutions to the challenges of deportations, the clogging of asylum applications and regularisation of the Zimbabwean migrants whose population was now estimated at around 2 million (Amit, 2011). People from various classes managed to integrate into the South African community, find employment and create stable bases of livelihoods. Most of the respondents interviewed noted that they had lived in South Africa under the ZSPs for at least the past 10 years. Despite the considerable length of stay, it has been impossible for Zimbabweans to acquire citizenship through legal means. Most of the respondents who have been accommodated through the ZSP testified to a growing structural resentment towards their presence, hence most are outward looking. They are in a continuous search for new settlement destinations due to the impossibility of legally settling in South Africa. The case of Joel below gives some insights into the dynamics that are affecting most Zimbabwean Special Permit holders.

> "I came to South Africa in 2008 at the height of political violence and I had to seek asylum. I got lucky to get asylum and managed to find employment in Johannesburg. My asylum was changed to the ZSP and that is the document I have been using up to this year (2023) when my document expired. It has become increasingly difficult for me due to the daily challenges that you encounter without proper documentation. I applied

for another visa in August 2022, but I am still awaiting a decision from the Department of Home Affairs. It becomes scary especially that I have spent more than 15 years of my working life here and to go back and start again is difficult. I haven't travelled outside the country since applying for change of visa because I heard that if they see that you have gone back home it is an automatic rejection of the visa since it means that the political threats that I used to get asylum are no longer there".

Like many other respondents, Joel's story brought out the everyday struggles of migrant Zimbabweans in South Africa. Their lives are characterised by uncertainty and a continued structural denial of their abilities to integrate formally into the South African state. It has been impossible for the migrants to legally attain permanent residence in South Africa.

The DZP has also been noted to be largely feeding upon the inequality characteristics of the Zimbabwean migrant communities. The year 2023 has been regarded as the final year for the temporary special visa and Zimbabwean migrants have been advised to apply for alternative visas. This has the potential of fomenting illegality by designating people whose stay had been regularised as illegal foreigners. Mostly those with limited skills are finding it difficult to transition to other types of visas. At the same time, those that have applied for other visa types are still encountering challenges in relation to the delays in giving decisions to their applications. The evident state incapacity to give decisions points to various systematic problems. These include political balancing acts, where decisions towards migrants are a potential political campaign tool, especially in line with public perception towards African migrants. It may also point to bureaucratic incapacity, with the DHA claims being overwhelmed. Finally, the policy hesitancy may also reflect official prejudice against migrants that cannot be brought out through state policies. Bureaucratic procedures become handy tools of bottlenecking access to legality, hence forcing migrants to look for other destinations. Most of the respondents attested to the hostile bureaucratic environment that is making it difficult for them to process legal documents. One respondent had to travel from Johannesburg to Durban simply to be able to submit her application for a visa. She failed to get a slot at the

Johannesburg office and so it was better to book at the Durban office. This implies that resource constrained individuals may not possess the same economic flexibility, hence ending up being pushed into illegality.

The 90 Day Visitors Permit

Most migrant Africans in South Africa, especially in the SADC region, depend on temporary visas for their entry into South Africa. The temporary visa consists of a 90-day yearly allocation for holders of valid passports from selected countries. These are granted at the ports of entry without prior cumbersome applications. It involves the immigration officer stamping and allocating the required number of days on the traveller's passport. Due to circulatory migration characterised by individuals spending short periods of time in South Africa, most migrants use the temporary allowance to do business and return to their home countries. However, due to bottlenecks and challenges in the access to formal work visas, long-term migrants have used the same system to maintain a legal status in South Africa. The given days enable the migrants to go around policing agencies especially in areas where patrols for illegal migrants are rife. The temporary permits are also useful among families with a discordant legal status. Various situations could be seen where the working partner might have a valid permit whilst the spouse relies on temporary visas. Such was the case with Jonathan, a Zimbabwean migrant who managed to find work in South Africa. As someone who initially came without the family, Jonathan was able to apply for his work permit without the family members. His wife utilises the temporary visa to legally stay in the country. Their two young children are however part of the undocumented migrants since they were born in South Africa, but the legal status of their parents makes it impossible for them to access legal documentation in South Africa. They have managed to go back to Zimbabwe to register the births of their children though they have not been able to acquire travel documents yet. Although Jonathan and his family expressed a longer-term vision for himself and his family, their access to legality remains a nightmare that they must confront at various points of their stay in South Africa. They mostly live in fear and uncertainty induced by the precariousness of the family members' legal status. Jonathan articulated how at one point they had to keep their children indoors after rumours that police were rounding up migrant children in preschools and arresting their parents for being in the country illegally. Numerous other cases existed that showed the uncertainty, fear and stresses that came with being a foreign African migrant. Policing regimes and processes of legalising migration has resulted in the use of the temporary visa system to cope with the problems of failing to properly attain residence permits.

The liminality of Zimbabwean migrants has been cemented through systems of ensuring their temporary stay in South Africa. One mechanism through which Zimbabwean migrants have managed to enable their legal stay in South Africa has been using the 90-day port of entry permits. Most individuals who do not qualify to use the formal system utilise this process to ensure that they stay legal. Upon expiry of the 90 days, some go out of the country and re-enter so that they can be given more days. However, an elaborate system has emerged where individuals can send their passports and have them stamped. Networks of transporters and immigration officials are involved in the underhand deals of extending permits. Although this remains a stop gap measure, it remains evidence of the difficulties of settling in South Africa. It continuously creates a situation of temporariness for both skilled and unskilled migrants. The aspect of belonging become more complex in a situation where one is continuously conscious of their outsider-ness. Immigration officials and border control personnel have cashed in on the allocation of days, especially at land border posts, where they corruptly require a fee to give a traveller a preferred number of days. If one fails to pay, they are usually given up to a maximum of two weeks. The strict requirements on eligibility have resulted in practices that force African migrants to find innovative means of navigating legality and ensuring access to the South African space. However, others simply use the 90-day temporary stay as a mechanism of gaining entry. They then send their passports to be stamped as if they have exited the country hence rendering them part of the undocumented migrants. Some of the respondents have used the system to stay in the country for average periods of five to ten years. Legislation when restrictive produces regimes of illegality. When migrant prospects of real integration are curtailed, they would rather stay under the radar and navigate the daily challenges. However, this process creates and perpetuates migrant vulnerability and precarity.

Lesotho Special Permit

Whereas the state attempted to regularise the migration of Zimbabweans through the special permits under the ZDP, an almost similar project was implemented in trying to deal with migrants from Lesotho. South Africa is the first destination for all migrants from Lesotho due to its positioning. This has resulted in an influx of migrants from Lesotho into South Africa as most livelihoods are tied to migrant work activities in South Africa. In a bid to document the illegal Basotho migrants, the DHA initiated the Lesotho Special Permit in 2015 for work, study and open businesses (Makhata and Masango, 2021). The permits were changed in 2019 and extended to 2023. Similar to the ZSP, the Lesotho Special Permit can be seen as an attempt to curb illegality and improve state knowledge of migrants in the country. Most of the provisions have been temporary, with no avenues for naturalisation. Hence, the legal perspective can be seen to be instrumental in fencing the access to citizenship and creating a demarcation between South Africans and others. Such an approach fails to take into cognizance the different historical dynamics of interaction and migration patterns of Basotho into South Africa. Currently people are living without documentation and relying on the evidence of visa application. About 90 000 Basotho nationals were noted to be beneficiaries of the Lesotho Special Permit.

The Waiting Receipts

Migrant applications have fomented new dynamics of waiting. This situation cements feelings of transience and temporariness among migrants. Several respondents pointed out that they were uncertain about their future in South Africa although they had applied for different kinds of visas (Nyakabawu, 2021). Some respondents have been in the waiting mode for more than a year. This has forced an outward looking planning process among migrants as their hopes of remaining in South Africa continue to fade. As one respondent shared her thoughts, she had the following remarks to make:

> "I always look forward to pronouncements by the home affairs
> minister. You know when they say we can be in the country
> awaiting the outcome of my visa application, it gives me a little
> bit of time to plan the next few months. Though, there is this
> anxiety that always creep when I think of the future, there is
> a slight hope that we will be given an opportunity to continue
> being in South Africa. However, with the competition for jobs,
> we will eventually have to leave".

The remarks showed the implications of waiting for migrants. Migrants were torn between two worlds, where on one side the better prospects in South Africa created a desire for them to remain in the country, whilst at the same time the hostile legal environment created uneasiness and affected any assurance that they will be able to stay in the country for longer periods. Some respondents noted that they could only plan in line with the legal time that they have been given.

Waiting produces liminality. It creates a difficult environment for migrants, marked by limitations, fear, and anxiety. Narratives further strengthened fear and anxiety, as most migrants with who were awaiting the outcomes of their visa applications were switched into a temporary mode. One such experience was narrated by a respondent who had six months of waiting for her visa outcome. She narrated the difficulties associated with the fear of a negative outcome since it meant that she would immediately become an undesirable person in South Africa. To make matters worse, she read stories of others claiming that if one travelled back to their country whilst on the waiting period, the DHA would simply reject their visa application since it showed they had an option to go to. Despite her desire to visit her home country, she had to wait for an undefined amount of time so that she could stand better chances of regularising her stay in South Africa. The uncertainties produces by waiting affect the belonging of migrants and affects their ability to identify with space.

Conclusion: Rethinking Legality, Citizenship and Belonging

This Chapter explored the dynamics of legality and its relationship to contemporary experiences of belonging among migrant African in South Africa. The tool of policing migration, while important as a framework for controlling migration processes, is important in directing the flow of migration experiences. It contributes to belonging by being the first point of contact between the migrant and the state. It creates atmospheres of welcomeness or exclusion through the experiences that migrants have with the official mechanisms of handling migration. There is a legalistic regime that seeks to define the real South African and simultaneously provide a clear and unambiguous identity regime. Through tightening the process of who can become a South African, the state has been instituting legal and policy frameworks that bar access to citizenship. A look at the Zimbabwean and Lesotho experiences show that the legal and regulatory frameworks are not aimed at aiding but at abetting the citizenship of African migrants. There is a granting of temporary permanence, one that gives the migrants a reprieve as they prepare for inevitably going back to their areas of origin. As noted by current experiences where the migrants from both Lesotho and Zimbabwe have to apply for alternative visas, it shows that the traditional expectations of accessing citizenship are unachievable. Migrants can spend more than ten years jumping from one visa to another without a chance of ever being accepted as legal citizens of South Africa.

Legality based citizenship is complex and has proven to be a quagmire for the South African state. Although the state has a desire to be in control of the process of who can gain access to South Africa, the existence of illegal migrants has been a constant headache that is not the traditional basis of accessing citizenship. Whilst laws and policies have attempted to keep African migrants out, the examples of Zimbabwe and Lesotho show that the state has to be forced to bend its rules as it responds to the practicalities of containing migrant practices. The moratorium on migrants from these two countries shows the difficulties of handling migration flows and point to the importance of an analysis of practice for to understand the dynamics of citizenship.

Citizenship also points to bundles of rights that individuals enjoy by being members of specific societies (Naujoks, 2020). The Zimbabwean case has shown the difficulties that the state faces in instituting measures of exclusion as migrants have used the state's judicial system to ensure that they fight for inclusion and rights of staying in South Africa. Zimbabwean migrants have continuously appealed against state attempts to terminate their temporary permanence by ending the rights given by the ZSP. Migrants have won the case for continued stay, reflecting the complexities associated in attempting to ring-fence access to citizenship. Although citizenship generally affords rights to individuals who have been given the rights to the state, it has been noted that even those considered outsiders have the capacity to access rights within the same jurisdiction where they do not belong through appealing to the supranational instruments of rights and morality. Citizenship is negotiated, providing both insiders and outsiders with an opportunity to discursively build a discourse on citizenship. The legal definition of citizenship is in crisis due to the rise of quasi-citizenship forms, that make it difficult to implement the rules of exclusion. Nevertheless, the citizenship of African migrants is highly contested, with the state frustrating avenues that can give access to legal citizenship.

Whilst this chapter has explored the legal and policy dimensions of accessing citizenship for foreign African migrants, we acknowledge that these do not constitute the totality of experiences citizenship and belonging. The interaction of foreign African migrants and the host communities constitutes another prism for understanding the belonging of foreign African migrants in South Africa. The next chapter explores the dynamics of community experiences of the migrants as they navigate the everyday contexts of the host communities.

Chapter 5

Navigating belonging: Community experiences of foreign African migrants

This Chapter explores ideas of belonging by analysing how foreign African migrants navigate the daily experiences of living in South Africa. The daily navigation of the South African landscape produces discourses of practice that shape belonging. Although citizenship is important in shaping the dynamics of belonging, it is the daily living that influences whether the migrant feels accepted in the community where they settle. Citizenship affords the migrant rights to a place, but it fails to include the totality of belonging since this is a qualitative emotional aspect that is based on the attitudes of both the migrant and the hosts.

Belonging is shaped by several features that include, physical/geographic location, culture, and identity. Being in a place creates frameworks for emotional attachment and feelings of being. These are influenced by how the individual becomes integrated into the host communities. This Chapter notes that migrants have usually adopted three behavioural dispositions. These include assimilation, dualisation and rejection. On assimilation, migrants attempt to integrate themselves into the existing cultural dynamics of their host communities. These include participation and the mimicry of host communities' way of life. Dualisation on the other hand involves a syncretic approach that involves borrowing internal cultural configurations whilst simultaneously keeping the migrant's own cultural lifestyles. The extreme aspect has been that of rejection where migrants are simply in the foreign land but living according to their own home cultures that bear little connection to the locality. These migrants have high levels of exclusivity, only interacting with local communities within professional circles. Their social and cultural belonging is influenced more by their places of origin, and they have managed to create their migrant islands, divorced from the day-to-day aspects of their host communities.

Belonging is also shaped by interactions in the public space. As foreign African migrants navigate the societies they live in, there is a creation of practice that shapes belonging. The Chapter notes that interactions in various spaces produce feelings of inclusion and exclusion. These feelings are influenced by the extent to which the migrants feel welcome and accepted within the host community. Whilst Chapter 4 explored the legal side of citizenship by focusing on instruments of compliance with the legal regimes of movement, this Chapter broadens the concept of citizenship to accommodate the obligations and expectations on the part of the migrant. Citizens require access to services, and a means of earning a living regulated through the existing governance frameworks. However, the Chapter shows that the situation for African migrants in South Africa is complex and sometimes chaotic. They can have access to legal documents but experience restrictions when it comes to accessing the labour market. The tag of a foreigner has implications on their experiences in the economic, social, and political spaces of the country. Hence it is argued that there is a dual process of making and unmaking of the migrant citizen. This process is located within time and continuously evolves to mirror existent political and socioeconomic dynamics in South Africa. The making and unmaking of the citizen constitute one duality among others that show partial inclusion and exclusion of the migrant. It reflects a simultaneous and ambivalent process of acceptance and rejection of the African migrant. It also produces other dualities that include the formal and the informal. These dualities have a bearing on belonging for the African migrant and produces different attitudes and perceptions towards migrant assimilation into foreign spaces. From the study, various aspects shaped the experiences of foreign African migrants. These include the access to financial and banking systems, the labour market and workplace dynamics, living conditions and access to accommodation, as well as general interactions in the public sphere.

Banking System

Citizenship affords individuals access rights to the economic infrastructure found within the state since the state is the regulatory instrument structuring financial flows. The ways through which migrants' financial experiences are structured influences their perceptions of belonging. One sector that appeared to be important has been the banking system which is seen to influence the flows of money in the lives of migrants. The banking system is important in shaping how migrants transact daily within South Africa, as well as shaping circles of remittances and foreign transactions. Narratives from several respondents describe their experiences in terms of access to financial resources, including home and car financing as well as how this has shaped their perceptions and feelings of belonging. The story of Sophia illustrates the challenges encountered in dealing with access to the banking systems. She noted multiple times when her accounts were arbitrarily frozen because of her foreignness. This happened on occasions when her visa expired, and she was awaiting renewal. The other time was when her lease agreement that she used as proof of residence had lapsed so the bank froze her accounts as they waited for her to supply a new proof of residence. The inconveniences caused by sudden denial of access to financial resources was a significant reminder of otherisation for Sophia.

Another respondent, Geoffrey, narrated the harrowing experience that he encountered on opening an account. His case brought out the difficulties that migrants face not only in relation to getting legal access to South Africa, but also in accessing public services. Geoffrey wanted to revive his dormant account with a local bank. He received his visa late and it only had three months left out of the one year that he had applied for. The teller was reluctant to help him arguing that the DHA had advised them that they were not releasing visas. The teller was questioning the authenticity of the visa as well as the limited time that remained. After the intervention of Geoffrey's nephew, who was fluent in local languages, he was finally assisted, and the teller gave him a month to ensure that he provided a new contract and proof of application for a visa. The financial restrictions can be seen to be a burden on migrants and often relates to a question of belonging. Being an outsider becomes difficult as migrants must often prove their legitimacy and eligibility to participate in both economic and social spaces. Migrants are often excluded from the ease of access to the banking system, resulting in numerous informal transactions where migrants employ surviving tactics to be able to transact. These informal transaction channels are high risk and exorbitant, often charging a big percentage for migrants to be able to send money.

Banking system regulations also affect the saving patterns of migrants. They influence the rates at which migrants opt to use formal banks as portals for both savings as well as investment portfolios. Financial inclusion is crucial for the migrant's ability to sustain a livelihood and acquire assets. Most migrants who had access to finance were able to enter into loan agreements enabling them to buy properties and motor vehicles. This class of migrants showed a greater inclination towards assimilating and blending into communities, since their ability to participate fully in the financial sector improved their long-term planning. This was contrary to migrants with temporary residence permits, whose uncertainty of tenure created feelings of temporariness and uncertainty. Moreover, their documents did not allow them to participate fully in the economy since they could not access resources such as lines of credit and assets financing schemes. For illegal immigrants, the situation was worsened by their inability to access formal channels of economic transactions. One respondent narrated how he had to plead with a businessperson to use his account for receiving payments from his clients.

> "When I get a contract, I give the customer my friend's account and he will withdraw the money and give me cash to use. It is risky and at times I must give him some money to thank him for the service. It becomes more difficult for me to deal with my clients directly and in the process, I lose from the extra charges I incur. I am simply planning to get enough money to purchase equipment then I will return home (home country) and invest there".

These observations reinforced the importance of financial inclusion in creating a sense of belonging. Financial inclusion enhanced one group's desire to plan long term whilst the other group were in a temporary mode due to their inability to fully participate in the South African economy.

The Workplace

Workplace dynamics are complex. the diversity that the migrants bring to the workplace presents complex configurations to the migration experience. Daily workplace interactions are a point of contact between migrants and locals and their daily interactions contribute significantly to the quality of the migration experience. Dynamics of inclusion and exclusion are evident from the levels of both the hiring of workers and promotions, as well as workplace practices. These dynamics shape the migrant's feelings of belonging as they determine the degree to which the migrant finds acceptability and comfort within the local community. Whereas people create relations of conviviality as they work together, there are degrees of inclusion and exclusion that structure workplace relations for foreign African migrants in South Africa. The length of period at work may determine the level of inclusion and cooperation characterising daily interactions in workplaces. However, various situations create complexities that have a direct impact on the belonging of migrant workers. To understand workplace dynamics, it is imperative to explore three processes that include recruitment and selection, the workplace dynamics of daily interaction and promotions and separation from organisations due to the end of contracts, retrenchments, or other factors. Identity, although not the only important factor, usually comes in handy in the experiences of different categories of workers.

Legality has implications on employability. It constrains the individual navigation of the South African society through stifling the individual connections to formal institutions and from transacting properly. This has the net effect of worsening migrant conditions as they become informalised. These immigrants cannot even afford to stand up for their rights and often end up having informal work arrangements where they are susceptible to abuse and being underpaid. They often live in fear, without access to legal recourse as they are usually hesitant to come out and face the possible consequences of having their legal status discovered. One female respondent noted that she worked for a white owned restaurant and left with her employer owing her a full year's salary. They would simply get allowances to let them get to work and sometimes pay bills whilst their full salary remained unpaid. Attempts at getting legal recourse were futile due to the expenses of legal representation and the migrant identities which significantly diminished any public sympathy towards the ill-treatment of migrant workers. The works precarity characterising foreign African migrants are further discussed in this Chapter.

The designation of migrants as last resort choices for employment creates a system that results in the economic disenfranchisement of the migrants. As noted in Jason's case, there are both official and unofficial tendencies towards making the hiring of migrant workers more difficult, even to those who possess formal South African documentation. This has a net effect of pushing migrant African foreigners into informality and occupation of largely insecure jobs. As noted by the STATS SA survey from 2012-2017, there have been more regional migrants in informal sector jobs when compared to South Africans. This points to an official alienation that affects belonging due to the limited space for migrants in the South African economic space. During fieldwork, several holders of permanent residence permits who were either underemployed or out of work were encountered. Many also noted that they had attended numerous interviews but seemed to be unable to cut into the labour market. Some respondents blamed the equity provisions which they noted as having no space for foreign African migrants. Employment patterns, underpinned by transformation and decolonisation uses a hiring system that prioritises groups which were formerly discriminated against. These include women and people with disabilities as well as black Africans. As one respondent noted: '

> "The person who has a high chance of being employed is the black South African woman, followed by the black South African man and other racial groups based on their historical conditions. There is no migrant African in that equation and you can only get employed when truly no one can be hired for the job. Migrant African foreigners have a pretty difficult time attempting to find work".

One migrant narrated his story where the temporary position that he occupied was advertised to become a permanent post. During the interviews he managed to come out on top although his foreignness became an issue with the appointing authority. They decided to offer a South African born individual the job and had to reluctantly offer him a temporary position so that he could orient and mentor the local. He noted that they promised him a contract only on condition he would transfer his skills to the South African. Despite having permanent residence, accessing permanent work positions were a bit challenging. The respondent noted that he was at an advanced stage to relocate to America where he had secured a job. The workplace proved to be an arena for the fight over belonging where the nature of an individual's legality was instrumental in shaping chances at acquiring long term contracts. Roots were important in influencing acceptability in workplaces with local born Africans standing a greater chance of being employed.

Although navigating the public space has been easier through the acquisition of the relevant *lingua franca*, interactions in the world of work point to the difficulties that migrants face. Migrants like Jason could navigate the South African society with ease due to different advantages coming from an intimate knowledge of communities. However, Jason's problems were in relation to the formal system, where systemic salience of difference has systematically side-lined him from acquiring posts commensurate with his skills. He noted that he only got contracts with the longest being one year despite having a South African I.D. and required qualifications. He says:

> "No one gives you permanent contracts anymore. My I.D show that I was not born in South Africa hence it is easier for me to be sidelined and posts would be given to South Africans born in the country. Though I am legal here, I do not enjoy the benefits and for the past three to four years, I have not been able to land any permanent post".

The system of identification that categorises migrants according to their origin has resulted in a systematic discrimination against migrants, regardless of their legal status. Jason professed tiredness with the legal system and is contemplating a move to Canada. The limitations on the rights of foreign African migrants creates elements of temporality and are a perpetual reminder of the outsider designation that they occupy. Although daily interactions may sometimes be devoid of the problems of constant feelings of otherisation, various instances of contact with the formal system results in experiences of foreignness among the migrants. As noted in Jason's case, one can formally be in the country but experience limitations in relation to access to certain resources in the public arena. There is an unmaking and otherisation of the migrant through perpetual reminders that their origins are not South African hence they should not expect equal opportunities and treatment as compared to South African born people.

Work dynamics could be seen to cut across both the formal and informal arena of employment. Irrespective of their skill set, some migrants experienced anti-foreigner sentiments in the working environment. Whilst the unskilled migrant workers bore the brunt of prejudice and sometimes bad labour practices characterised by underpayment and late payment of salaries, the skilled ones found shrinking spaces of leveraging their skills for employment. One respondent in higher education noted how he was asked to change his visa from a critical skills visa to a visitor's visa if he wanted to get a position at a university. This was akin to downgrading his visa and take one that was more restrictive and, in a way, removes him from the path of attaining naturalisation. The African migrant is not only the last choice but despite possession of skills, they face other dimensions of exclusion that impact their ability to naturalise and their belonging. Despite being highly skilled, the respondent bemoaned his treatment by the organisations that he interacted with. He confessed to mental strain resulting from prejudice and discrimination both in the workplace and within society at large.

Some of the issues that employed African migrants experienced included complex labour practices that often were characterised by identity undertones. One respondent noted how he was persecuted and was eventually laid off, even though he had attained a South African permanent residence permit. He noted that it was both stressing and difficult for him as he had to endure discriminatory practices in the workplace. To compound the situation, he was laid off soon after taking out a mortgage in one of the affluent suburbs, hence a sudden loss in income was difficult for him. He noted that the permanent residence permit was important for him in securing employment and finding legitimate spaces in South Africa. However, the qualitative aspects of belonging were deeply affected by negative experiences as well as situations that always reminded him of his foreignness. His professional development and better income became important aspects in motivating the respondent's resolve to soldier on, regardless of the negative workplace experiences.

Living Conditions

The issue of living space is one of the major factors that bring together migrants and the host communities. Living space by its nature is shared, and this implies that most daily interactions between migrants and host communities is witnessed in the living spaces. Moreover, migration dynamics often result in migrant concentration in specific neighbourhoods of the host communities, depending on the various socioeconomic dynamics of the migrants. These daily interactions are also seen to be important in shaping the inclusion and exclusion of migrants. They therefore contribute to the feelings of belonging among the migrants. One migrant, Tafara, had well established connections when it came to securing welding jobs in Durban. Although he did not have access to proper banking platforms, he relied on other migrants' access to banking. His connections with the community allowed him to secure jobs and referrals, and he even managed to teach informally at one of the local vocational training centres. To adapt, he also learned the local languages and even picked a local isiZulu name that made it easier for him to appear 'part of the community'. Community integration was important for acceptability and belonging. It made it easier for migrants to share their life experiences with hosts in proximity. Migrants could get neighbours, friends, and networks through residence dynamics. However, this differentiated with location, with those who lived in the low-income high-density areas exhibiting better levels of integration than those who lived in affluent spaces characterised by more anonymity.

African migrants residing in lower income areas and informal settlements were also more susceptible to attacks during times when tempers flared due to different reasons. As foreign Africans were the softer targets, they bore the brunt of public anger at a dysfunctional society characterised by poverty and inequalities (Van Hout and Wessels, 2023). Competition produces conflict, hence competing access to space especially in informal settlements created a mixture of identities. Foreign African migrants were even accused of sneaking their way into benefitting from RDP houses, which South Africans felt should only be occupied by locals. Even some foreigners who leased or sold the RDP houses created tensions and exposed foreigners to attacks from South African who felt entitled to be the sole beneficiaries of these houses. Hence it is evident that economic inequalities shaped spaces for belonging, with competition over resources resulting in different regimes of exclusion. It heightened the instinctual protectiveness that individuals feel when they have perceptions of being under threat.

The Public Sphere

The public sphere presents another space for the appreciation of migration dynamics. The daily interactions in the public sphere carve specific configurations on citizenship and belonging. For migrants, traversing the daily public sphere creates patterns that create feelings of attachment to place. Experiences in the public sphere include contact with law enforcement, transacting with locals, and other facets such as transportation and interactions with locals. It includes flows of information and ideas within the public domain (Habermas, 1997; McKee, 2005). This renders two dimensions of the public sphere. The first is an abstract intangible space, or domain where ideas and information as well as public debate take place. The second attempts to capture interactions and behaviours among individuals in the public space. Habermas (1997) discusses both mediated and unmediated public spheres, where the mediated spaces involve the interaction of ideas and information, often mediated through social media platforms. The unmediated aspects of the public sphere can also be seen through daily interactions among individuals. This is crucial for producing both public opinion on migration as well as for creating praxis or discourses of interaction that enable the understanding of the behaviour of migrants. This section explores how daily interactions influence discourses of citizenship and belonging, and also how public opinion expressed through social media debates, popular protests, and media content addresses the issues of the citizenship of foreign African migrants.

One peculiar aspect of the public sphere is the role of language as a currency that enables easier navigation. Language as a tool of communication is important in understanding dynamics of interaction and physical encounters in public spaces. Comprehending a language makes it easier to transact in the public sphere, especially for a foreigner. An interesting observation was noted by one respondent who pointed out how being black often makes people assume that you understand local languages, hence they will most often start conversation in the prevalent language. The respondent noted that sometimes when they are served in shops, personnel address them in local languages although when they witnessed the same personnel attending to White, Coloured, or Indian individuals they will automatically switch to the English language. Their shared skin colour creates expectations of sameness and once the migrant speaks, it automatically shows their foreignness. Language becomes more than a medium of communication, but an asset for migrant access to the community and resources. A comprehension of the local *lingua franca* is important for talking oneself out of situations. Language limitations increase one's alienation in public spaces through limiting conversation, and inversely improves their position if fluent in local languages. Having conversations with some African migrants, they recounted an impasse in the bank when the teller was reluctant to help one of the respondents to regularise their bank account. It took the negotiating skills of the nephew who was fluent in the local Sepedi language to break the impasse and get the required assistance. Police checks, access to public services and even getting assistance in public spaces is shaped by understandings of language.

The public sphere also creates an impression of belonging by enabling a view of migrant interactions with local sociocultural activities. During discussions with one of the respondents, the issue of soccer came up and the respondent noted that although he is an avid soccer supporter, he did not feel any attachment to the South African teams, preferring to support his home team even during matches with South Africa. He noted that when South Africa hosted the World Cup, he was clad in the colours of his home team that he was cheering on, despite having South African citizenship. His emotional loyalty lay with his former country rather than showing an allegiance to the country that had afforded him citizenship. There is a complexity of transforming long term internalised convictions and embracing new values due to changing citizenship. Public discourse on migration has created an exclusive South African society, which in turn results in resistant ideologies and behaviours as migrants respond to exclusion in the public space.

Ideas and emotions about migration experiences in the public sphere presents a window into understanding issues of belonging. The authors also interacted with some content on social media platforms, specifically Facebook, WhatsApp, and X. Fraser (2014) notes the importance of public platforms like the social media in building public opinion of migrants thereby shaping experiences of belonging. These three sites carry rich information on the daily experiences of migrants and even the perceptions of hosts towards migrants. They were taken as platforms to vent frustrations and discuss experiences from the perspectives of both the migrants and host communities. Cloaked with a degree of anonymity afforded by social media, individuals often interact and share extremist views in relation to migration. There is a significant rise of social media accounts that denigrate African migrants and pursue content that portray migrants in a bad light. In the same vein, some of the platforms become arenas for action to mobilise individuals and advocate different issues in relation to migration. It includes frustrations with the handling of migration, and at the extreme end there are physical acts directed at migrants. One popular movement has been operation Dudula, that has predominantly conveyed anti-migrant sentiments and has engaged in activities bordering on vigilantism. In a recent interview by the BBC, some individuals born in South Africa but with a foreign parent were dragged in by disgruntled members of operation Dudula as they labelled them foreigners. The public sphere is capable of redefining what constitutes citizenship and often runs discourses parallel to official legal and policy provisions. However, the public sphere is also a social gauge of the sentiments in communities especially in relation to migration issues. An analysis of the evolution of operation Dudula shows the rise of a social movement bent on transforming the migration dynamics of South Africa. although it has emerged as a part of disgruntled citizens responding to perceived excesses, criminality, and illegitimate benefitting from resources by migrants, operation Dudula is transforming from vigilantism to a political party whose manifesto is built on correcting the injustices and negative aspects of migration.

The public sphere has thus produced discourses of public opinion with certain prejudices against foreign African migrants. This includes labelling different nationalities and associating them with specific criminal and illegal behaviour, including drug trafficking, muggings, invading the second economy/informal sector, and usurping employment opportunities, among others (Nhemachena, Mawere and Matapuri, 2022). The public sphere can influence policy, as law and policymakers, respond to the social gauge that the public opinion will have created. There has been no prominent action taken by the state towards addressing individuals fomenting xenophobic attitudes or publicly acting outside the law to attack migrants. The cases show that African migrants bear most of the anti-migrant sentiments, hence creating an alienation that affects belonging. Most respondents in Gauteng confessed to have experienced some form of exclusion and negative attitude due to their foreign origin. The public sphere also shapes the emergence of a specific perception of a migration problem, with sensationalisation becoming part of the perceptions towards migration. Social media platforms and even some public media have been responsible for creating and sustaining an impression of South Africa being overrun by migrants. There has been a stoking of fears based on perceptions of negative aspects that a 'migrant infestation' may bring. In the public space, scary statistics show that migrants sustain fears of a migrant takeover. The public sphere shapes the preparedness of the South African communities to welcome the citizenship of African migrants. The process is complex and ambiguous, characterised by both embracing and rebuttal. However, in the public sphere, the voice that carries the day is usually the voice of fear and exclusion. Across the world, the evidence of opposition to migration has been louder than situations of inclusion, with the case of Brexit being one of the contemporary manifestations of the closure of migration spaces and the prevalence of anti-immigrant voices.

Informal livelihoods

Informality is one of the major adaptive mechanisms for individuals who fail to penetrate the formal markets. It presents an important livelihood source for most migrants, especially the irregular migrants whose incorporation into the formal sector is restricted by the documentation requirements. During fieldwork in Gauteng and KwaZulu-Natal it was noted that most migrants could be seen engaging in informal economic activities like recycling, construction, housework, informal trading, welding, and crafts, among others. Most of the jobs depended on their negotiating skills as they were key to accessing clients. Hence, it was noted that most undocumented migrants survived through greater integration with the host communities so that they could access jobs. Rather than the professional whose work was shielded by the comfort of the office, and who seldom used public transport, the undocumented migrant's survival is pinned to their ability to integrate into the host community for access to various resources. Hence the social citizenship of undocumented migrants showed greater levels of belonging than those of the legal migrants.

Intercultural Relations and Experiences

One of the major issues affecting issues of citizenship has been the aspect of multiculturalism. Proponents of multiculturalism advocate the embracing of diversity by appreciating the differences that exist between people. However, migration discourses have tried to advocate a monoculture by requiring migrants to integrate into host communities. As noted by one permanent resident, some of the requirements for citizenship in South Africa include the migrant's ability to understand one local language, establish relations with other South African citizens who can offer testimonials to support applications, and to demonstrate the value that one brings into the country. Hence, there are elements of producing homogeneity and advocating assimilation through processes of integration. Contemporary commentary on anti-migrant discourses argue that multiculturalism has been a failure and is in disarray. Recent remarks by the British Home Affairs minister, ironically a product of migration, reinforce growing antimigrant sentiments based on the idea that the diversity brought by migrants has been a threat to local cultures and values. Similar sentiments have been shared in South Africa, that migrants are not respecting locals and continue to undermine the sociocultural values of the host communities. This creates difficult situations of general unwelcomeness of migrants and paints them as the embodiment of the erosion of the social fabric of host communities. These sentiments also further alienate migrants forcing them to group together in enclaves where they retreat into their own communities of comfort.

The enduring nature of identities and cultural values also makes it difficult for African migrants to feel a full emotional attachment to migrant destinations. Most respondents noted stronger existing ties to their home countries through familial links that always kept them in touch with home. However, some respondents also noted diminishing social ties especially if they had weaker ties with their extended families. As one respondent noted: '

> "I came with my family, and there is no one at home. We never
> had the rural ties and have fewer close relatives. For the past
> ten years we have gone back home only four times. My life is
> here and so is everyone who matters to me"

Such experiences showed a growing category of migrants whose roots were slowly becoming enmeshed in South. African society. Their emotional attachments and relations were identified more with their contemporary communities rather than with their home communities. The feelings and stability of immigration status was an important determinant in cultivating such sentiments, since most of the individuals who felt 'at home' in South Africa were those who had been able to successfully regularise their stay.

The aspect of intermarriages has also been a thorny issue in migration discourses. Marriages of convenience have been performed where foreigners, mostly men, take local wives for the purpose of acquiring citizenship, only to abandon them after regularizing their stay (Hobden, 2020). This has driven the state to try and legislate the marriage process in an attempt to stop marriages of convenience. However, this process has proved complex due to the difficulties characterising attempts at legislating interpersonal relationships. The process has been abused from both sides, with local women sometimes inheriting wealth acquired during their marriage to foreigners. Hence the idea of marriage sparks a complex set of emotions towards intercultural relations between locals and foreigners. In interviews the authors managed to speak to several foreign African migrants who were married to locals. Their experiences showed greater attempts at identifying with local communities, although in some cases there were tensions, especially on the side of the foreign partner.

> "I have been slow in comprehending the language of my wife
> and imagine we are at a family gathering and I become the
> stranger in the family. People switch to their mother language
> and can make conversation with me occasionally but mostly I
> feel out of place when it comes to family gatherings".

Intermarriages have sometimes been sources of conflict with kin, especially due to the traditional distrust of marrying people from a different cultural group. One Zimbabwean respondent narrated how his uncles and brothers abandoned him and gave him an ultimatum to leave his South African wife if he wanted to maintain relations with them. Ironically the pressure was emanating from the people who were instrumental in facilitating his migration into South Africa. Hence these were important figures in his life. However, his wife was also important as she had been instrumental in bringing stability to his life through taking care of him during his days of financial struggle. It was an emotionally charged situation, and great tension existed due to the intermarriage. In their defense, the relatives exhibited a stereotype of local women as treacherous, often leaving their foreign husbands after wiping out their earnings hence they saw no future in the marriage. Examples were given by prominent people like the popular footballer, Tendai Ndoro, whose properties were allegedly taken by his wife after a fallout, leaving him a pauper. After a successful stint with one of the local football clubs, the player was able to buy high end vehicles as well as a mansion and these were said to be registered in the name of the wife. The wife was able to take all the possessions whilst the player returned to Zimbabwe empty handed. Historical memories of when migrants from Zimbabwe worked for several years never to return, returning empty handed, or coming back dead, presents traumatic experiences which create sentiments opposed to taking wives in South Africa. Hence there is a great opposition to intermarriages with locals as relatives fear that they are going to lose out as the married person may never be able to make meaningful investments back home. The underlying perception of South Africa as a temporary place where people are simply supposed to earn a living and invest back home dominates the mindsets of most migrants whose historical ties with South Africa, were characterized by circulatory labour migration. Marriage is something which brings permanence and is integral to families and clans. It is thus taken as an important step which should not simply be left to individual choices but should maintain familial ties and strengthen the whole clan. This creates a dilemma for migrants who want to achieve citizenship through marriage either consciously or unconsciously, as such decisions may not go down well with the expectations of their families leading to extensive resistance, as shown in this case. On the other hand, the respondent had professed stronger bonds to the spouse coupled with a desire to keep his family together, even to the point of telling off his relatives. Intercultural relations remain an important avenue in the understanding of migrant belonging.

The relationships established through friendship, marriage and other forms of acquaintanceship are important in understanding the conditions that structure either integration into local communities or maintenance of stranger-ness in local contexts. There is evidence that some African migrants have been to establish long lasting relationships with local people through intermarriages. These marriages have been instrumental in shaping acceptability and feelings of belonging for some African migrants. On the other hand they have been sources of discomfort due to intercultural experiences which often produces conflict. Cases have also emerged where migrant African foreigners enter into marriage amongst themselves in South Africa. In such situations there are expectations of South Africa as a place of permanence, as both migrants have left their original homes. This produces truly transnational families with limited ties or weakened connections with their places of origin. These new families often encounter several problems in relation to their intercultural experiences. Neither belong to the local cultures and at the same time both have diverse cultures from their places of origin, bringing a melting pot and interesting dynamics into the upbringing of their children. Their experiences of legality are also complex, considering the ever-changing conditions in relation to not only their citizenship but also the citizenship of their children. The mere fact of having children born in South Africa does not guarantee the citizenship of such children as different conditions in relation to the legality of their parents are considered in applications for citizenship. As noted by Hobden (2020) there is a tightening of the citizenship acquisition that results in the statelessness of children and may affect the rights of access to resources to which citizens are entitled.

Another form of citizenship amongst migrants has been a religious citizenship. Religious belief systems, especially Pentecostal Christianity, exhibited some mechanisms through which migrant Africans created their own versions of citizenship divorced from legal and community membership-based citizenship. By appealing to a God-given citizenship, migrant Pentecostal Africans subscribed to the view that wherever they are God has given them an opportunity and right of belonging. The resistance and exclusion that these migrants faced were taken as part and parcel of the cost of inheriting the land which

God had given to them. African Independent Churches, for example the Johani Masowe Wechishanu, popular among Zimbabwean migrants, also performed rites which strengthened the resolve of migrants to take on the challenges associated with being in South Africa. Hence rather than tying their belonging to the experiences which they faced, they believe in appealing to a greater citizenship which was given by their God. This gave them entitlement to space, despite the legal and practical challenges associated with being a foreigner in South Africa. Religion therefore functioned as a form of resistance ideology, strengthening and encouraging individuals by giving them a divine basis for belonging which was not based on what individuals dictated but on what God declared. This type of religious ideology was prevalent among migrants and helped them to cope with the uncertainties characterised by their existence in South Africa. Religion also seemed to be a common denominator in some spaces as they were able to unite migrants and hosts and one purpose as believers. Some of the respondents in Pretoria noted how they were given a church building to perform their services free of charge by members of their community in Soshanguve. This proved to be one cross cutting factor which led to individuals laying aside their differences and were brought together by practices of worship.

Conclusion

This Chapter focused on the experiences of belonging by foreign African migrants as they encountered different spaces of interactions in South Africa. There are several perspectives that have been noted in relation to citizenship and belonging. The platforms that mediate belonging have been examined, and these structure the experience of belonging. An examination of everyday spheres of interaction is important in understanding citizenship and belonging. Access to financial spaces, workplace dynamics, and the ideological and practical aspects of the public sphere are important in determining migrant attitudes and experiences of belonging. There are three main elements that can be summarised from this observation. These include access to resources, earning a living and public interaction dynamics. These shape the belonging and inclusion of foreign African migrants. It should be noted that African migrants compete for resources, ideologies, and space, and this influences their connection to migrant spaces. Whilst others have been able to integrate and gain acceptance in their host communities, other migrants have maintained separate spaces and often exhibit elements of alienation from migrant spaces. Although they occupy the migrant spaces, their visions and desires are outward looking, giving the impression that their contemporary migrant space is nothing more than a compromise with what they would have hoped for. For other migrants, South Africa presents the dream destination, hence there is an internal satisfaction and attempts to integrate into the communities at whatever the cost.

The Chapter also notes that citizenship in South Africa is fought on two fronts which are the legal perspective as well as the practical community perspective. Whilst Chapter 4 discussed legal issues, this Chapter extends citizenship beyond the mere achievement of legality and discusses the issues of acceptability that migrants often encounter in their day-to-day lives in migrant spaces. Without resorting to economic determinism, it is inescapable for migrants to engage in discourses of and negotiating citizenship with locals, and the issues of resources in their various manifestations become important in determining the acceptability of outsiders. Perceptions and attitudes towards migrants are built on experiences of contact between South Africans and migrant African foreigners. The ways of interaction determine how communities and citizens perceive the newcomers, with problems of society often being attributed to the presence of all foreigners. Broad based alliances with South African citizens are constructed on social networks, religious belief systems, and other forms of familiarity that weave the migrants and their host communities together. Cooperation in economic activities is noted between migrants and locals, as in the case of Zimbabwean migrants in Gauteng who are involved in the business of recycling. In KwaZulu-Natal there is notable cooperation between skilled migrants and locals who became part of the students in practical activities such as welding and construction. Relationships which bring mutual benefits between hosts and migrants are important in shaping the acceptability of the migrants in host communities. Cultivating synergies with locals can be seen to be important in enhancing the integration into host communities.

Having explored the everyday experiences of belonging, the next chapter provides an analytic lens for viewing the belonging of African others in the South African context. It combines both the experiences with the legal sphere as well as the public sphere and attempts to provide a coherent viewpoint of the identity and belonging of the African others in South Africa. The chapter also provides a framework for understanding the issues that are raised in the book.

Chapter 6

Concluding remarks:
Can an African Migrant become a South African citizen?

Introduction

Citizenship has been shown to entail various aspects. It has implications for the formal rights and obligations of the migrant. It also includes an assessment of the individual's integration into the civic life within a state. Access to legal protection and recognition by law are important elements in a migrant's life. However, the process of belonging is completed by importing the qualitative aspect of emotions, participation and acceptability tied to place. Full migrant integration is experienced in circumstances where the migrant should be able to have feelings of home. There are several aspects that affect the feelings of home that have been explored in this book. One of the factors includes the persistence of otherness among foreign migrant Africans. Identity by its nature presents enduring markers of difference that may become emphasised during different periods of the migrant experience.

The Policy Framework and Migration Practice

The policy framework governing migration is continuing the trajectory of exclusion and tightening access to the South African society. Whilst this is understandable in the context of socioeconomic crisis in the nation, it should also be seen as a misapplication of solutions stemming from a misdiagnosis of the problem at hand. Recently, the state commissioned the Border Management Authority, with the express objective of attempting to tighten the entry of undocumented and undesired migrants into South Africa. Calls for stiffer penalties for companies that employ illegal foreigners are also increasing, with legislation underway which ensures the tightening of the space for undocumented foreigners. Although moves such as these are paraded as targeting undocumented foreigners, in practice they set the stage for a specific mood towards foreign African migrants. The constant need to prove legality becomes part and parcel of a migrant's life. As noted by some respondents in the Gauteng province, you cannot afford to wander without your passport as it can be requested at any time by law enforcement looking for undocumented migrants. Although further away such as in KwaZulu-Natal, these experiences are rare, Gauteng was the place of focus for most migrants, resulting in more policing. The major point to note is that perceptions and experiences are moulded by existing practices that structure attitudes towards foreign African migrants.

The tightening of the policy thrust towards migration affects all facets of citizenship. It is creating perceptions of hostility towards African migrants hence reinforcing their feelings of exclusion from the South African society. Apart from the border policing discussed, the book has noted that processes of acquiring legality are becoming increasingly difficult. The state is increasing measures to keep people out and at the same time ensuring that those already in the country have done so through the correct procedures. There has been a tightening of bureaucratic procedures and centralisation meant to make it easier for lower levels officials to simply give legal rights to different levels of stay in South Africa. In the post Covid era there were more centralisation measures, and at one particular moment foreign missions of the state were not authorised to process visas, with everything forwarded to the DHA in South Africa. This ultimately led to visa delays, where foreign Africans both in South Africa and those who applied from their home countries were waiting ridiculously long periods to receive the outcomes of their visa applications. Several respondents noted how they were given their visas or decisions sometimes after more than eight months, whilst some are still waiting for the decisions. There are operations also to weed out officials who facilitate the acquisition of legal documents through clandestine measures. This should be understood also in terms of the difficulties that are put in place for individuals to acquire documentation. Some of the cases showed that some people could qualify for visa categories although the systemic hostility resulted them in paying huge sums of money to get their documents through corrupt avenues.

The existing policy regimes can be seen to contribute to feelings of temporality among African migrants. It becomes difficult to develop feelings of belonging in a space where they face multiple levels of exclusionary experiences. This fuels and reinforces feelings of being in South Africa but not belonging there. Despite various situations of belonging, there is an evident feeling of alienation amongst African migrants. Resistance discourses have emanated which appeal to the different identity factors used as the justification for remaining in South Africa. Africanicity, liberation history, blackness and even religious beliefs have been some of the rallying points shaping resistance discourses among migrant African foreigners. These add weight to their claims of belonging and enable them to cultivate feelings of belonging despite the evident hostile environment.

Contemporary Migrant Experiences

Migrant experiences are varied and there are interesting dynamics structuring the experiences of African migrants in South Africa. Migrants have to deal with the shrinking state in an ever-closing space for the citizenship of foreign Africans in South Africa (Hobden, 2020). From legislation to hostile communities and the closing down of space for migrants, contemporary patterns of migration experiences are characterised by the rejection of citizenship for Africans. Migrants must adapt and look to various strategies to ensure they secure their access to the South African society and economy. Contemporary legal battles waged by organisations like the Helen Suzman Foundation championed the rights of migrants against a political labelling process which looks at all accommodation and sympathy for migrants as evidence of being anti South African. Whereas negative perceptions and actions towards foreigners is interpreted as xenophobia, local narratives also paint the acceptance of migrants as evidence of betraying the goals of real South Africans. Hence movements like operation Dudula, and online based campaigns such as #PutSouthAfricansFirst, #ForeignersMustGo and #WeWantourCountryBak are advocating the marginalisation of migrants and the prioritization of South African citizens (Nhemachena, Mawere and Mtapuri, 2022; Tarisayi, 2021; Dratwa, 2023; Van Hout and Wessels, 2023). Vigilantism has seen the birth of violence and killings based on hate and fears spread by such movements that are pinned on xenophobia but there is little evidence and information of serious sanctions that deal with such incidences. The seeming impunity with which xenophobic and vigilante activities are characterised gives feelings of collusion and underlying acceptable social sanction. It appears as if the state is casting a blind eye, thereby inadvertently accepting vigilante activities. Political actors are also using migration as a rallying point for their political campaigns, with several groups promising stricter anti-migrant stances. There is an evident scapegoating towards migrants, whilst one political party has risked going against populism by advocating African unity and embracing foreign African migrants by appealing to a common African identity.

The situation of shrinking citizenship characterises contemporary migration experiences. Official and unofficial platforms exude an air of anti-immigration and the marginalisation of foreign African migrants. The civic space has also been dominated by a crop of citizens inclined to the strict enforcement of citizenship and the expelling of foreign African migrants through closing the spaces for living and earning livelihoods. There is a concerted desire to emphasise differences and for the enforcement of a denial of the rights for migrant African foreigners. Although personal experiences differ across the wide range of migrants and different nationalities, most people have had experience of the hostile side of citizenship characterised by the denial of their rights and the systematic exclusion of non-citizens. It is against these configurations that migrants have to negotiate their belonging. Through appealing to different mechanisms, migrants attempt to carve out their belonging through either an acceptance of the temporariness of their migrant situations, and a learned helplessness where migrants keep on hoping for benevolent policies allowing them continued stay in and access to the South African state. The second option is characterised by migrants popularising and strengthening their cause for belonging through using existing legal avenues and launching court challenges to counter exclusionary decisions by the DHA. Hence there is an emergence of a militant citizenship coming through a resistant body of migrants staking their claims of belonging in the South African spaces. Different other mechanisms such as mutual aid, social networks and even religious beliefs are all instrumental in crafting claims of belonging to South

Africa, and give migrants a renewed force to fight for a space in the country.

Balancing Home and the Foreign Space

One outcome of the belonging experience among African migrants has been an unending hope of a future return to their places of origin. Despite the varied levels of legality, a considerable part of migrant African foreigners looked forward to a future return to their countries of birth. Some migrants who had managed to buy properties were seeing these as investments that will give them an opportunity to earn an income when they go back to their countries of birth. Fewer African migrants exhibited enduring commitment and allegiance to the South African state, choosing to view themselves as temporary residents. They rather exhibited the desire to leave South Africa at a particular point in time, hence the maintenance of ties with home. Rather than viewing citizenship as a tool that evokes feelings of belonging, citizenship appeared to be a tool that is instrumental in negotiating access to the South African society and its resources. It allowed migrants to have the rights of legal stay and granted better access to formal economic spaces where they could earn a living. It was thus unsurprising for migrants to maintain and oscillate between migrant spaces and their original home spaces. Intra-household activities, including ways of socialising young family members, the communities, and groups which families interacted with, showed conservative, inward-looking patterns of existence among migrant communities, something that is antithetical to blending in and becoming part of the local South African communities.

Issues of identity become complex when citizenship is not clear or is characterised by difficulties in adapting to local communities. The cases of families and individuals whose citizenship was characterised by ambiguity is an important pointer to the difficulties of identity and belonging. This was noted in the case of the family where the father had acquired a South African permanent residence permit and had children born here but decided to go back to his home country to register these births. These are complicated identities which evolve where there is a troubled citizenship. When there is clarity and a sense of belonging, migrants are comfortable with establishing their lives in foreign spaces, but when there are complexities, they remain torn between loyalties and confused identities. Citizenship extends beyond mere legality and the presence of an individual in a place, regardless of the time spent there, may be inconsequential to their identity formation and their belonging. Hopes for future reverse migrations reinforce the individual oscillations of maintaining two homes, the migrant home and the original home of their birth. There is an evident promotion of trying to foster and cultivate home cultures, even in foreign spaces. This is through instilling origin cultural values in the children of migrants, and is something that places a barrier to full integration into migrant communities. The question of who is the South African has been asked mostly from a perspective of exclusion and barriers to the acquisition of citizenship. However, it is noted that the question must also answer the willingness and readiness of foreign African migrants to be part of the South African society. Apart from the challenges highlighted, is there a willingness to blend into host community cultures? Rather a persistence of home identities among migrants is seen, with most maintaining their original cultures, values, customs, and other identity aspects of their original migrant places. Hence the issue of belonging has limitations. It places the question on both the host and the migrant. Whilst host actions are important in creating an environment of welcome and acceptability, the migrant's willingness to adapt to the cultural configurations and aspirations of host communities should also be analysed.

Constructions of home are complex. Although they have been linked to qualitative factors like comfort, most African migrants are in migrant spaces out of necessity, thereby making these spaces more of survival and livelihood supporting destinations. The idea of home becomes secondary since the primary drivers of contemporary migration is migrant survival and earning a living. Despite the historical circumstances influencing movement, it is undeniable that contemporary migration in a way is linked to livelihood sustenance. This makes questions of belonging secondary, whilst the primary desire is to maintain a living. The resistance discourses that motivate migrants to stay put are based on a cost benefit analysis of whether to move or to stay in their country of birth. Temporariness hence becomes a factor that results in some migrants attempting to balance home and migrant spaces as they hope for a future return. Despite the totality of life experiences being based in the foreign space, there is an enduring feeling of foreignness that does not only emanate from the experiences in migrant spaces, but is born out of a mental and ideological construction of home as the space where one was born. The migrant space becomes home because of what it can offer, whilst the place of origin is home because of how belonging is constructed around feelings of a place shaping one's existence and being the space where one was brought up. Hence, even after satisfying legal requirements, the socio-cultural citizenship of foreign African migrants remains complex.

Revisiting Theorising Migration

One of the interesting observations has been the theoretical aspects of migrant experiences. Migration as a process brings a melting pot of experiences. However, most of the issues border on understanding inclusion and exclusion within different levels of migrant and host lives. Legal, social, cultural economic and political arenas are subject to spaces of observation for inclusion and exclusion between migrants and hosts. Most of the behaviours that occur between these binaries are reducible to the understandings of how migrants and hosts compete and complement each other in these spaces. Whilst it is convenient to label hosts as xenophobic and Afrophobic, a step back will allow a gaze that penetrates the veils of conflicts as emanating from competition over inclusion and exclusion. The very idea of citizenship is built upon creating identities that can be used as instruments of inclusion and exclusion. Resources are at the centre of migrant struggles. Their positioning in relation to these resources determine their welcomeness. That can explain why legal citizenship is underpinned by the benefits that the migrant can bring. The migrants are afforded stay if they are proven to positively contribute to the South African society, either by exceptional skills, investments, or proof that they have resources and income that enable them to avoid burdening the host community. The social contribution through relations such as marriage can be understood as the outsider becoming part of the family of insiders, hence allowing them to a earn their place in the South African society.

Theoretical analysis should go beyond labelling the surface

96

manifestation through exposing the underlying currents shaping behaviours. Citizenship and belonging are basically issues of inclusion and exclusion and how these play out is dependent on multiple aspects of both migrants and hosts. Perceived benefits are an inescapable aspect shaping this dynamic. Resistance towards foreign African migrants is built upon perceptions of them being a burden. The state labels them economic migrants, a term invoking elements of people who are economic refugees. This label blurs the distinction between legal and illegal foreign African migrants, leading to a denigration of anything labelled African and foreign.

The issue of identity is also important in theorising migration. The question of how migrants construct their identities has been seen to be important when attempting to have a wholesome picture of the dynamics of belonging. As noted in Chapter 5, some migrants choose to blend in whilst some outrightly reject this and proceed to protect their own separate identities. They do not blend in but choose to maintain their originality in a foreign space characterised by attempts to influence outsiders to blend in. The survival of foreign communities of migrants, often divided by places of origin, are crucial indicators on the enduring nature of identity and how it creates obstacles in relation to belonging. There are even social sanctions towards migrants who attempt to blend in, as other people in their migrant communities denigrate behaviour that mimics host peoples and communities.

Whilst it is attractive to portray migrants as victims of constraining terrains of negotiating citizenship, a real look at strategic essentialism enables an understanding of migrant responses to the constraining spaces of shrinking citizenship. By resorting to various strategies of challenging the state and communities, migrants themselves have empowered their groups to forcefully claim space in South Africa. Seeking asylum is one process that demonstrates migrant capitalisation of their helpless status to circumvent legality requirements in South Africa. Although the majority of migrants may not qualify for legally acquiring South African citizenship, alternative strategies to negotiate belonging are used to claim space in South Africa. Although migrants may not have entitlements to legal coverage in the migrant spaces, they are able to negotiate their belonging and assert their rights in South Africa by appealing to international standards such as human rights. Designation of categories such as economic refugees or economic migrants, although they seem to limit avenues for the acquisition of South African citizenship, are instrumental in giving migrants access to the South African spaces. This is done through appealing to the vulnerability which the migrants face, hence it would be inhuman for the state to simply close off access without affording the migrants a chance. Looking at the Zimbabwe and Lesotho examples, it can be noted that migrants have been able to establish their lives in South Africa for more than a decade, utilising their vulnerability context.

The Citizenship of African Migrants

The citizenship of African migrants in South Africa can best be described as a melting pot. This book has attempted to put this into perspective and organise trends and underlying perspectives that structure the citizenship for African migrants. Issues of legality are key to understanding the frameworks governing the belonging of African migrants. Through understanding the legal framework and the regulation of migration, official perceptions towards African migrants can be seen. It is undeniable that in the contemporary periods restricting their access to the state, space and livelihoods can sum up the anti-migration trends and sentiments in official circles. At the same time, these sentiments are cloaked by justifications of trying to ensure that only those that are needed for the economy may find space. However, an analysis of the experiences of people with the required skills show that the majority have found the process of legality as cumbersome, complex and demotivating, something that creates a generally hostile environment for migrants. Hostility to the foreign African migrant thus produces discourses of illegality as migrants attempt to find space in the South African society. It also produces prejudicial behaviour, as the migrants become the embodiment of anything negative and a symbol of the failures of the state. The rise of vigilantism, which has seen individuals harassing migrants, threatening and even killing them. That presents a complex picture against which migrants should negotiate their belonging in South Africa.

The readiness of South Africa to welcome the citizenship of foreign African migrants is increasingly limited. Official channels for proper documentation and acceptance of migrants are characterised by bottlenecks and frustrating experiences, consciously or unconsciously driving down their interest in settling in South Africa. Given an option, most respondents highlighted that they would not think twice about choosing a different migration destination. However, viewing migration from the top by focusing on legal channels may miss the everyday innovations of migrants in carving out a stake in the South African state. Although statistics give the official picture of attempts at achieving formality, there is a larger body of migrants that live under the radar of official authorisation and laws. They make use of unofficial channels or use backhand strategies to circumvent official regulation. They access the same institutions that citizens are entitled to through using different mechanisms which may include community integration, faking of documents and even corruptly paying for access to different gatekeepers existing in South African communities.

Despite the security upgrades and tightening movement and entry of migrants, even undocumented migrants use the same channels designed to exclude them by corrupting them to facilitate their access. Everyday interactions of individuals create networks and bonds that stimulate belonging and acceptance of the belonging of African migrants. One strategy by anti-migrant activists was to arrest or penalise landlords and employers who gave space and employment to illegal migrants. This shows how micro processes can circumvent the seemingly impermeable terrain of citizenship in South Africa. These processes are instrumental in producing dual systems of inclusion and exclusion, where on one side familiarity and conviviality build relations and community between migrants and foreigners, whilst at the same time also breeding resentment and targeting for discrimination. This was seen in the Gauteng xenophobic attacks where the intimate knowledge of foreigners' residence exposed them to raids by local vigilante groups (Oxford Analytica 2022). Although political rights are limited, illegal migrants gain access to other provisions by belonging to different communities, hence creating the ability to survive in South Africa. At the same time, a look at the formalisation of citizenship through examining legal processes shows that legality does not ultimately confer citizenship. Instead, official recognition is a step that ushers an individual into the arena of negotiating citizenship through daily interactions in different platforms such as workspaces, the public sphere and other arenas that bring migrants into contact with situations that require them to prove their identities.

Directions for Further Research

Migration is a permanent feature of contemporary societies. As different conditions shape the existential conditions of individuals, people will always be on the move for different reasons. The issue of belonging is a crucial aspect that requires further examination. With the simultaneous processes of globalisation and localisation, population circulation continues to structure several aspects in relation to inclusion and exclusion and how communities and countries can deal with the issue of integrating migrants into their communities. This book focused on the experiences of foreign African migrants, although they do not constitute the only group that is on the move. There is a need to further explore the differential experiences of other racial groups as they migrate into African spaces. Global geopolitics point to an increase in relations with nations from other continents like Asia. This is likely to increase the presence of Asians in Africa and hence it is important to explore their experiences and their belonging to see how they compare with African migrants.

The host communities also remain the most important dynamic in the citizenship and belonging experience. Major political and socioeconomic dynamics continue to influence attitudes and predispositions towards migrants. An exploration of changing local political and sociocultural configurations and how they are instrumental in shaping the migration experience is therefore recommended. Although looking at citizenship and belonging, the focus has mainly been on telling the story from the perspective of the migrant, although it is important to ensure that both the migrant and host perspectives are properly captured. A further analysis of the local dynamics and host experiences with migrants is necessary to understand how these shape citizenship and belonging. Of note is the increase in social relations with foreign African migrants, something that results in an enmeshing of identities. As relations develop and evolve, there is a blurring of the lines that demarcate groups into the 'us' and 'them'.

Finally, regulating migration is another aspect that needs further exploration. Measures of population control and regulating access by migrants continue to be an important aspect of managing migration. The book recommends an exploration of the ideological basis of migration management and a further understanding of the ways in which migration policies and attitudes are shaping the regulatory environment of migration. It should be noted that as societies progress, new challenges are likely to arise that shape the migration dynamics of communities. Understanding the patterns and integration of migration is an important step towards efficient migration management. Human societies are difficult to include rigid boundaries, as seen through the various citizenship actions of migrants in South Africa. This calls for alternative ways of conceiving, perceiving, and handling migration flows. Resources are lost in the misplaced measures of containing and directing population movement. The understanding of migration dynamics is therefore crucial for better processes and planning.

References

Agamben, G. and Sacer, H., 1995. Sovereign power and bare life. Homo sacer, 1.

Ahmed, S., 2000. Who knows? Knowing strangers and strangerness. *Australian feminist studies*, 15(31), pp.49-68.

Akanle, O., Alemu, A.E. and Adesina, J.O., 2016. The existentialities of Ethiopian and Nigerian migrants in South Africa. *International Journal of African Renaissance Studies-Multi-, Inter-and Transdisciplinarity*, 11(2), pp.139-158.

Amit, R., 2011. *The Zimbabwean documentation process: Lessons learned.* African Centre for Migration and Society.

Amit, R. and Kriger, N. (2014) "Making migrants 'il-legible': The policies and practices of documentation in post-apartheid South Africa", Kronos Vol.40 n.1 Cape Town Nov., African Centre for Migration & Society, University of the Witwatersrand Federal Research Division, Library of Congress, Washington, DC.

Barker, V., 2012. Global mobility and penal order: Criminalizing migration, a view from Europe. Sociology Compass, 6(2), pp.113-121.

Barth, F., 2010. Introduction to ethnic groups and boundaries: The social organization of cultural difference. Selected studies in international migration and immigrant incorporation, 1, p.407.

Batisai, K., 2022. Retheorising Migration: A South-South Perspective. In Migration in Southern Africa: IMISCOE Regional Reader (pp. 11-24). Cham: Springer International Publishing.

Belvedere M. F. (2008), "Contested Identities and the politics of Refugees in Post-apartheid South Africa", A paper presented to the FMSP-IFAS conference on The State of International Migration Studies in Southern Africa, 17-19 March, Johannesburg.

Bentham, J., 2020. *The panopticon writings.* Verso Books.

Bilchitz, David & Ziegler, Reuven., 2023. Is the automatic loss of South African citizenship for those acquiring other citizenships constitutional? Democratic Alliance v Minister of Home Affairs, South African Journal on Human Rights, DOI: 10.1080/02587203.2022.2158925.

Bourbeau, P., 2011. The securitization of migration: A study of movement and order. Taylor & Francis.

Breakfast, N., Bradshaw, G. and Nomarwayi, T., 2019. Violent service delivery protests in post-apartheid South Africa, 1994-2017 – a conflict resolution perspective. African Journal of Public Affairs, 11(1), pp.106-126.

Breckenridge, K., 2005. The biometric state: The promise and peril of digital government in the new South Africa. Journal of Southern African Studies, 31(2), pp.267-282.

Candiz, G.O. and Bélanger, D., 2019. The politics of 'waiting' for care: immigration policy and family reunification in Canada.

Carmel, Rickard (2015)"Refugee wins asylum after 10 years in legal limbo," Mail & Guardian February 27.

CDE., 2011. "Introduction" in South Africa's Migration Policies, A regional perspective, Centre for Development and Enterprise (CDE), Workshop No. 8, February.

Chekero, T. and Morreira, S., 2020. Mutualism Despite Ostensible Difference: HuShamwari, Kuhanyisana, and Conviviality Between Shona Zimbabweans and Tsonga South Africans in Giyani, South Africa. Africa Spectrum, 55(1), pp.33-49.

Connerton, P., 1989. How societies remember. Cambridge University Press.

Crush, J. (1997) Temporary Work and Migration Policy in South Africa. [Available at: www.polity.org.za:80/govdocs/green_papers/migration/crush2.htm. Accessed on 12 June 2023].

Crush, J. and Chikanda, A., 2012. The third wave: Mixed migration from Zimbabwe to South Africa.

Crush, J., Williams, V. and Peberdy, S., 2005. Migration in southern Africa. Policy analysis and research programme of the Global Commission on International Migration.

Dekoke, T., 2016. Congolese migrants and South African language appropriation. Language Matters, 47(1), pp.84-104.

DHA., 2017. White Paper on International Migration for South Africa, July, Department of Home Affairs, [Available at: https://www.intergate-immigration.com › blog › latest-…,Accessed 11 June 2023].

Dorman, S., Hammett, D. and Nugent, P., 2007. Introduction: Citizenship and its casualties in Africa. In Making Nations, Creating Strangers (pp. 1-26). Brill.

Dratwa, B., 2023. 'Put South Africans First': Making Sense of an

Emerging South African Xenophobic (Online) Community. Journal of Southern African Studies, 49(1), pp.85-103.

Eide, E. (2016). Strategic essentialism. *The Wiley Blackwell Encyclopaedia of gender and sexuality studies*, pp.2278-2280.

El-Haj, T.A., 2019. Making and Unmaking Citizens: Law and the Shaping of Civic Capacity. U. Mich. JL Reform, 53, p.63.

Fraser, N., 2014. Transnationalizing the public sphere. John Wiley & Sons.

Foucault, M., 2008. Panopticism" from" discipline & punish: The birth of the prison. *Race/Ethnicity: Multidisciplinary Global Contexts*, 2(1), pp.1-12.

Foucault, M., 2023. Discipline and punish. *In Social Theory Re-Wired* (pp. 291-299). Routledge.

Gordon, J., 2022. In the zone: Work at the intersection of trade and migration. *Theoretical Inquiries in Law*, 23(2), pp.147-183.

Haklay, M.M., Dörler, D., Heigl, F., Manzoni, M., Hecker, S. and Vohland, K., 2021. What is citizen science? The challenges of definition. The science of citizen science, 13.

Handmaker, J. and Nalule C. (2021) Border enforcement policies and reforms in South Africa (1994-2020) The International Institute of Social Studies, Working Paper,No. 686, July.

Handmaker, J. and Parsley, J., 2001. Migration, refugees, and racism in South Africa. Refuge, 20, p.40.

Heater, D., 2006. Citizenship in Britain: A history. Edinburgh University Press.

Hunter, E., 2016. Citizenship, belonging, and political community in Africa: dialogues between past and present. Ohio University Press.

Hobden, Christine (2018) Report on Citizenship Law: South Africa, Global Citizenship Observatory (GLOBALCIT) Robert Schuman Centre for Advanced Studies in collaboration with Edinburgh University Law School, February.

Hobden, C., 2020. Shrinking South Africa: Hidden Agendas in South African Citizenship Practice. Politikon, 47(2), pp.159-175.

Kavuro, C., 2021. Marriages of convenience through the immigration lens: concepts, issues, impact and policies. *Law, Democracy & Development*, 25.

Kinnvall, C. and Nesbitt-Larking, P., 2013. Securitising citizenship:(B) ordering practices and strategies of resistance. Global Society, 27(3), pp.337-359.

Klaaren, J. (2008), Citizenship Policy Through the Apartheid Ages, Paper presented at the IFRAS/FMIS international colloquium on The State of International Migration Studies in Southern Africa, 17 March 2008, Wits University.

Klaaren, Jonathan (2000), "Post-Apartheid Citizenship in South Africa" in From Migrants to Citizens: Membership in a Changing World edited by T. Alexander Aleinikoff, Douglas Klusmeyer (eds.) Washington DC: Carnegie Endowment for International Peace.

Klaaren, Jonathan. (2010) 'Constitutional Citizenship in South Africa', International Journal of Constitutional Law 94(8) pp. 94 -110.

Klotz, Audie (2000) "Migration after apartheid: deracialising South African foreign policy", Third World Quarterly, Vol. 21, No 5, pp. 831–847

Kochenov, D., 2019. Citizenship. Mit Press.

Kornegay, F.A., 2006. Pan-African citizenship and identity formation in Southern Africa: An overview of problems, prospects, and possibilities. Johannesburg: Centre for Policy Studies.

Landau, L., 2011. *Contemporary migration to South Africa: a regional development issue*. World Bank Publications.

Landau, L.B. and Bakewell, O., 2018. Introduction: Forging a study of mobility, integration and belonging in Africa. Forging African communities: Mobility, integration and belonging, pp.1-24.

Lemanski, C., 2020. Infrastructural citizenship:(de) constructing state–society relations. International Development Planning Review, 42(2).

Lonsdale, J., 2016. 14 STATE AND PEASANTRY IN COLONIAL AFRICA. People's History and Socialist Theory (Routledge Revivals), p.106.

MacDonald, A.S., 2012. Colonial Trespassers in the Making of South Africa's International Borders 1900 to c. 1950 (Doctoral dissertation, University of Cambridge).

Makanda, J., 2016. *South Africa and peacebuilding in the Democratic Republic of Congo (DRC) 1996–2016: probing the attitudes of Congolese refugees in Durban* (Doctoral dissertation).

Makhata, M.B. and Masango, M.J., 2021. Illegal migrant Basotho women in South Africa: Exposure to vulnerability in domestic services. *HTS Teologiese Studies/Theological Studies*, 77(2).

Makina, Daniel (2011) "Zimbabwe: Migration patterns and political strife" in SOUTH AFRICA'S MIGRATION POLICIES, A regional perspective, Centre for Development and Enterprise (CDE) Workshop no 8, February.

Malope, Lesetja (2019) Foreigners and business permits: What the law says, City Press, 15 May [Available at: https://city-press.news24.com/ accessed 12 June 2023].

Manby, B., 2009. Citizenship law in Africa (p. 58). Open Society Institute.

Makina, D. and Mudungwe, P., 2023. Patterns and Trends of International Migration within and Out of Africa. In *Routledge Handbook of Contemporary African Migration* (pp. 79-98). Routledge.

Maphosa, France (2011) "Lesotho and Botswana: Small countries, pourous borders" in South Africa's Migration Policies, A regional perspective, Centre for Development and Enterprise (CDE) Workshop No. 8, February.

Marcus, G.E., 1995. Ethnography in/of the world system: The emergence of multi-sited ethnography. Annual review of anthropology, 24(1), pp.95-117.

Martin, Philip (2011) "Global migration and lessons for South Africa" in SOUTH AFRICA'S MIGRATION POLICIES, A regional perspective, CDE Workshop no 8, February.

Masenya, M.J., 2017. Afrophobia in South Africa: A general perspective of xenophobia. Bangladesh Sociological Society, 14(1), p.81.

Maunganidze, O. N. (2021) Migration Policy in South Africa: Lessons from Africa's Migration Magnet for European Policymakers, edited by Victoria Rietig and Alia Fakhr, Institute for Security Studies.

McKee, A., 2005. The public sphere: An introduction. Cambridge University Press.

Habermas, Jurgen (1997) 'The public sphere', in Robert E. Goodin and Philip Pettit (eds) Contemporary Political Philosophy: An Anthology, Oxford: Blackwell Publishers, pp. 105–108.

Mhandu, J., Ojong, V.B. and Muzvidziwa, N.V., 2018. Modus operandi and the socio-spatial milieu in which immigrant niche markets vis-a-vis informal economic activities. Journal of Social Development in Africa, 33(2), pp.85-108.

Misago, J.P. and Landau, L.B., 2023. 'Running Them Out of Time:' Xenophobia, Violence, and Co-Authoring Spatiotemporal Exclusion in South Africa. Geopolitics, 28(4), pp.1611-1631.

Mosselson, A., 2010. 'There is no difference between citizens and non-citizens anymore': Violent xenophobia, citizenship and the politics of belonging in post-apartheid South Africa. Journal of Southern African Studies, 36(3), pp.641-655.

Moyo K and Zanker F (2020). South Africa's xenophobic agenda is impeding its coronavirus response. African Arguments. [Available at: https://africanarguments.org/2020/04/09/southafrica-coronavirus-xenophobic-agenda-impeding-response/, accessed 23 April 2023].

Moyo K. (2021) South Africa Reckons with Its Status as a Top Immigration Destination, Apartheid History, and Economic Challenges, Migration Policy Institute [MPI], November 18.

Muzondidya, J., 2010. Makwerekwere: Migration, citizenship and identity among Zimbabweans in South Africa. Zimbabwe's new diaspora: Displacement and the cultural politics of survival, pp.37-58.

Naujoks, D., 2020. Atypical citizenship regimes: comparing legal and political conceptualizations. *Comparative Migration Studies*, 8(1), pp.1-20.

Neocosmos, M. (2006), From 'Foreign Natives' to 'Native Foreigners''. Explaining xenophobia in Post-apartheid South Africa, Dakar, CODESRIA monograph series.

Nhemachena, A., Mawere, M. and Mtapuri, O., 2022. Operation Dudula, Xenophobic Vigilantism and Sovereignty in Twenty-First Century South Africa. Sovereignty Becoming Pulvereignty: Unpacking the Dark Side of Slave 4.0 Within Industry 4.0 in Twenty-First Century Africa, pp.153-174.

Nyakabawu, S., 2021. Liminality in incorporation: regularisation of undocumented Zimbabweans in South Africa. *Anthropology Southern Africa*, 44(1), pp.1-15.

Nyamnjoh, F.B., 2008. Souls Forgotten. African Books Collective.

Nyamwanza, O. and Dzingirai, V., 2020. Big-men, allies, and saviours: mechanisms for surviving rough neighbourhoods in Pretoria's Plastic View informal settlement. *African and Black Diaspora: An International Journal*, 13(3), pp.283-295.

O'reilly, K., 2022. Migration theories: A critical overview. Routledge handbook of immigration and refugee studies, pp.3-12.

Ojong, V. and Sithole, M., 2007. The substance of identity:

territoriality, culture, roots and the politics of belonging. African Anthropologist, 14(1-2).

Ojong, V. B, Ashe, M.O. and Otu, M. N. (2018) "The Different Shades of Africanity within the broader South African Identity: The Case of African Migrants", Journal of African Foreign Affairs. Vol 5. No. 2, Oct, 123-146.

Ojong, V.B., 2012. Pragmatic and symbolic negotiation of home for African migrants in South Africa. Alternation, 19(1), pp.262-279.

Ojong, V.B.A., 2005. Entrepreneurship and identity among a group of Ghanaian women in Durban (South Africa) (Doctoral dissertation, University of Zululand).

Oxford Analytica, 2022. South African vigilantes will target more migrants. Emerald Expert Briefings, (oxan-es).

Paalo, S.A., Adu-Gyamfi, S. and Arthur, D.D., 2022. Xenophobia and the challenge of regional integration in Africa: understanding three cardinal dynamics. Acta Academica, 54(2), pp.6-23.

Peberdy, S. (1997) The Participation of Non-South Africans in Street Trading in South Africa and in Regional Cross-Border Trade: Implications for Immigration Policy and Customs Agreements. [Available at: www.polity.org.za:80/govdocs/green_papers/migration/crossborder.htm Accessed June 05, 2023].

Posel, D., 2004. Have migration patterns in post-apartheid South Africa changed?. *Journal of Interdisciplinary Economics*, 15(3-4), pp.277-292.

Ramphele, M., 2001. Citizenship challenges for South Africa's young democracy. Daedalus, 130(1), pp.1-17.

Rugunanan, P. and Xulu-Gama, N., 2022. Migration in Southern Africa: IMISCOE Regional Reader (p. 270). Springer Nature.

Sadiq, K., 2008. Paper citizens: How illegal immigrants acquire citizenship in developing countries. Oxford University Press.

Sawa, S. M. (2016) The Impact of Immigration Policies on Socio-Economic Transformation of South Africa, mini dissertation submitted in partial fulfillment for the requirements for a Master of Law (LLM) Degree in Public Law, University of Pretoria.

Schama, S., 1995. Landscape and memory. (No Title).

Sibanda, N. and Stanton, A., 2022. Challenges of socio-economic mobility for international migrants in South Africa. Migration and Development, 11(3), pp.484-500.

Siddique, M. A. B. (2005) South African Migration Policy: A Critical Review, The University of Western Australia Business School.

Spivak, G.C., 1986. Imperialism and sexual difference. Oxford literary review, 8(1), pp.225-244.

Stasik, M., Hänsch, V. and Mains, D., 2020. Temporalities of waiting in Africa. Critical African Studies, 12(1), pp.1-9.

Tarisayi, K.S., 2021. Afrophobic attacks in virtual spaces: The case of three hashtags in South Africa. Migracijske i etničke teme, 37(1), pp.29-46.

Tarisayi, K.S. and Manik, S., 2019. The Role of Land Reform Beneficiaries and the Reasons for Them Developing and Supporting a Satellite School in Masvingo, Zimbabwe: A Social Capital Marriage of Nhimbe and Allied Reasons. Education as Change, 23(1), pp.1-18.

Tarisayi, K.S. and Manik, S., 2020. An unabating challenge: Media portrayal of xenophobia in South Africa. Cogent Arts & Humanities, 7(1), p.1859074.

Tati, G. (2015) The immigration Issues in the Post-Apartheid South Africa: Discourses, Policies and Social Repercussions, pp. 423-440 [Available at: https://journals.openedition.org/eps/3496#authors, Accessed June 10, 2023].

Tessier, K. (1995) The Challenge of Immigration Policy in the New South Africa, Indiana Journal of Global Legal Studies, Vol. 3, Issue 1.

Tewolde, A.I., 2020. Reframing xenophobia in South Africa as colour-blind: The limits of the Afrophobia thesis. Migration Letters, 17(3), pp.433-444.

Vandevoordt, R., 2021. Resisting bare life: civil solidarity and the hunt for illegalized migrants. *International Migration*, 59(3), pp.47-62.

Van Hout, M.C. and Wessels, J., 2023. # ForeignersMustGo versus "in favorem libertatis": Human rights violations and procedural irregularities in South African immigration detention law. Journal of Human Rights, pp.1-22.

Wegner, K.L., 2014. Can there be a global historiography of citizenship?. *Routledge Handbook of Global Citizenship Studies*, pp.139-149.

The book published by Routledge, focuses on the changing research methodologies in social science research, prompted by the new social world shaped by the pandemic. It explores adaptations and developments to meet the demands of transforming social circumstances and showcases innovative alternative approaches. Featuring a range of international and interdisciplinary contributors who discuss the context of social science research in the "new normal", the book sets out the need to redesign research to address present-day challenges for the post-pandemic.

The contributors to this volume were drawn from institutions around the world. They come from Oxford Brooks Business School, UK; Auckland University of Technology, New Zealand; KU Leuven's Faculty of Engineering Science, Belgium; Victoria University, Australia; Temple University, USA; Ontario Tech University, Canada; University of KwaZulu-Natal, South Africa; Johannes Kepler University of Linz, Austria; Yale University, USA; University of Wolverhampton, UK; Paris Lodron University Salzburg, Austria; and European Institute on Public Health Policy, Ukraine.